Interactive Internet

Available Now!

Build a Web Site: The Programmer's Guide to Creating, Building, and Maintaining a Web Presence
The CD-ROM Revolution
CompuServe Information Manager for Windows: The Complete Membership Kit & Handbook (with two 3½" disks)
Computers Don't Byte
CorelDRAW! 5 Revealed!
Create Wealth with Quicken
Create Wealth with Quicken, Second Edition
Cruising America Online: The Visual Learning Guide
Excel 5 for Windows By Example (with 3½" disk)
Free Electronic Networks
WINDOWS Magazine Presents: Freelance Graphics for Windows: The Art of Presentation
Harvard Graphics for Windows: The Art of Presentation
IBM Smalltalk Programming for Windows and OS/2 (with 3½" disk)
Internet After Hours
Internet for Windows—America Online Edition: The Visual Learning Guide
KidWare: The Parent's Guide to Software for Children
Lotus Notes 3 Revealed!
LotusWorks 3: Everything You Need to Know
Mac Tips and Tricks
Making Movies with Your PC

Microsoft Office in Concert
Microsoft Office in Concert, Professional Edition
Microsoft Works for Windows By Example
OS/2 Warp: Easy Installation Guide
PageMaker 5 for the Mac: Everything You Need to Know
PageMaker 5 for Windows: Everything You Need to Know
Paradox for Windows Essential Power Programming (with 3½" disk)
A Parent's Guide to Video Games
PC DOS 6.2: Everything You Need to Know
WINDOWS Magazine Presents: The Power of Windows and DOS Together, Second Edition
QuickTime: Making Movies with Your Macintosh, Second Edition
The Slightly Skewed Computer Dictionary
Smalltalk Programming for Windows
The Software Developers Complete Legal Companion
Software: What's Hot! What's Not!
SuperPaint 3: Everything You Need to Know
Think THINK C! (with 3½" disk)
Thom Duncan's Guide to NetWare Shareware (with 3½" disk)
Visual Basic for Applications Revealed!
The Warp Book: Your Definitive Guide to Installing and Using OS/2 v3
WordPerfect 6 for Windows By Example
WordPerfect 6 for Windows: How Do I...?

How to Order:

For information on quantity discounts contact the publisher: Prima Publishing, P.O. Box 1260BK, Rocklin, CA 95677-1260; (916) 632-4400. On your letterhead include information concerning the intended use of the books and the number of books you wish to purchase. For individual orders, turn to the back of the book for more information.

Interactive Internet

The Insider's Guide to MUDs, MOOs, and IRC

William J. Shefski

PRIMA PUBLISHING

Prima Publishing™ is a trademark of Prima Communications, Inc. P™ is a trademark of Prima Publishing, a division of Prima Communications, Inc.
Prima™ is a trademark of Prima Publishing, a division of Prima Communications, Inc.

Prima Online™ and design is a trademark of Prima Publishing, a division of Prima Communications, Inc.

Project Editors: Lisa Armstrong, Andrew Mitchell, Pattie Lesser

"Delphi Internet™" is a trademark of the Delphi Internet Services Corporation.

"SprintNet®" is a registered trademark of Sprint.

Prima Publishing and the author(s) have attempted throughout this book to distinguish proprietary trademarks from descriptive terms by following the capitalization style used by the manufacturer.

Information contained in this book has been obtained by Prima Publishing from sources believed to be reliable. However, because of the possibility of human or mechanical error by our sources, Prima Publishing, or others, the Publisher does not guarantee the accuracy, adequacy, or completeness of any information and is not responsible for any errors or omissions or the results obtained from use of such information.

ISBN: 1-55958-748-2
Library of Congress Card Number: 94-68670
Printed in the United States of America
95 96 97 98 AA 10 9 8 7 6 5 4 3 2 1

Dedication

For Luke and for Joe. Our sons.
"Number one. Can do. Peace. Victory."

The first systems…are always the most complex.
　　— Adam Smith, Essays on Philosophical Subjects (1795)

Acknowledgments

thanks to the contacts at those systems through which the bulk of the work for this book was accomplished: Rusty Williams at Delphi Internet; Terry Rossi, sysop of PICs Online!; and Michelle Tessler of Pipeline. To all those with whom I had contact in the course of this book, a big interactive network of thanks. Special notes of appreciation for Jennifer Smith (FAQ maker), Lydia Leong (MUD research maintainer), the Bartle brothers, Richard (MUD maker of MUD makers) and Roy (Art Maker); and to elusive netpal Evan Tapper, whose enthusiasm helped galvanize my commitment to this project and who then faded away with a faulty forwarding address. Tapp, wherever you are, take a short break from your "random good deeds." ET, phone home.

Table of Contents

Introduction

his book has its roots, as many seem to, in another book. That would be *Free Electronic Networks*, which was about a decidedly *non*interactive form of networking. Its subject was the BBS networks, run by average computer enthusiasts, from their homes mostly. These systems pass their users' messages perhaps once per night, on short hops around the country and the world. It's a leisurely pace, but when I first came across them, I knew I was onto something. So it was with the MUDs. I first experienced a Multiple User Dungeon (or Dimension), while casting a wide research net for that first work. I attended a final class session, held online at Massachusetts Institute of Technology's Media MOO, for a course called "Sociology of Cyberspace." The class, though, was an offering of UCLA, across the continent, in that Fall of 1993. Fumbling with the unfamiliar commands may have inhibited my enjoyment of the actual conference—in which 15 students and Prof. Peter Kollack, the instructor, sitting at terminals in Los Angeles, discussed the state of the social networks with a like number of invited guests, MOO passers-by (watching on MOO TV) and network experts. As with the initial exposure to the BBS networks that launched in Free E Nets, so did that first MOO experience result in the quite strong feeling that, "Hey, I think there's something here."

The MOO was the opposite of the echo networks. Interaction was in real time (lag permitting), as if your computer had come alive. This parallels the sense that one gets while popping into any interactive environment on that vast interlaced worldwide computer network. Those around you—those with whom you can discourse and argue and chat and work—

may project their presence from anywhere on Earth. Spend enough time on the networks and you won't fail to run across the newcomer, or even a jaded old-timer, who, despite the touted non-expressiveness of a mostly text environment, cannot easily mask a sense of awe. At times the words go unuttered, at times paraphrased along the lines of "Hey, I think we're onto something."

For all the good press given the World Wide Web of late, with its dizzying hypertext links and potential for spreading of democratically generated information, it is not much of a way for connecting with *people*.

The more interactive resources on the Net are the MUDs and the IRC channels, many of which may hold no interest, but a few of which plainly illustrate that the future of this technology lies in connecting live people with each other, whether one at a time, or in globally distributed hordes.

Chapter 1

What Is MUD?

did that tree say something? Was that a nuclear missile flying overhead? Is that my class starting? Am I late for that meeting?

There are Multi-User Dimensions (MUD) where all these events may occur—meetings, classes, warfare and, yes, trees that *ask* to be hugged. These *textual* environments (some go by the acronym MUSE, for Multi-User Simulated Environment) may be the sleeper application of the technological networking watershed through which we now pass.

MUDs offer gaming in the role-playing mode, some fantasy, some cyberpunk, some neither. Some MUD-makers are exploring unusual or exotic topics from history or fantasy. You may come across some places where everyone seems to be dressed up as a cartoon animal. Strange. Yet, to each his own.

There are the more serious MUDs, used for education or professional networking—though serious is merely a relative label applied for the contrasts these environments create with gathering places *IRL* (In Real Life). So-called *serious* MUDs have no shortage of informality, whimsy and liveliness.

A dichotomy has arisen—as dichotomies always seem to do—between the gaming MUDs and the *social* MUDs—those that have become meeting places for primarily non-game activities. The software is evolving along these separate lines. Gaming MUD forms allow "killing" of characters (or *p-killing* as its called, short for *player killing*). Newcomers on these

MUDs, which make no allowance for the inexperienced, will find them dangerous and frustrating places, with the newbie serving as little more than experience point fodder for the entrenched, stone-hearted early comers. Some social MUDs have no such violent commands available.

The game MUDs offer questing, with the goal usually a rise up through higher ranks, and the garnering of privileges. Indeed, when *wiz* (wizard) status is attained, it usually carries with it the attainment of MUD programming powers. This is the coveted ability to change the virtual environment by having access to the programming language on which the environment depends.

There are many offshoots of the MUD concept. One of these families of variations is called MOO, for MUD, Object-Oriented. MOOs offer a high degree of programming flexibility—with business cards, vehicles and familiars (objects that can be sent on chores like observing the action in another room or delivering messages). This lends itself to an interesting, though somewhat surreal, environment for socializing and discussing business. First, though, a bit of explanation.

A MUD is a computer program that applies the principles of shared memory to the act of communications. Users *telnet* into the host computer, usually. Telnet is the Internetworking protocol that serves as the standard by which the connected computers understand each other. Telnet is part of the large bundle of such protocols that make up the widely accepted computer networking system called TCP/IP, the Transmission Control Protocol/Internet Protocol. This set of agreements (protocols) comprise the base on which the informal cloud of networks known as *The Internet* rests.

Telnet is the portion of TCP/IP that allows any computer to speak to any other in real time, from a distance. If you have a computer with telnet installed—or if you can call a computer that allows telnet—you can then visit many of the hundreds of MUDs out there in the Net.

Gaining Access

Being able to touch a computer a half-world away may be one of the most refreshing rushes available legally in this or any country. Sure, it's amazing that you can call friends overseas or across a continent, but the cost is daunting for anything but the most terse verbal exchange. With the computer communications system that arose from a government and educational research project, you can command and manipulate computer resources that might be located anywhere on earth (perhaps, someday, beyond). The network is so efficient compared to other methods that even if you're using a home computer with a modem, you may be able to access all of it with a local call.

For many individuals associated with a university or a business that links its computer network to the Internet, access is no problem (though rules, regulations and work-or grades-related strictures might be). In large organizations such as these, terminals abound and resources are plentiful, to the point where some users lose sight of costs involved and their access takes on the appearance of free Net time. It is not free. The equipment and wiring that link it all must be bought and maintained, and because the Net is nearing its capacity, there are indications of tightening of resources.

Still, access is no problem for those with the inclination. The skills necessary are becoming less arcane. The commercial providers in the recent surge have the added incentive of making their ports to the Net easier to use. This is a point of competition and incentive which is never felt by universities and industrial research facilities. Also, the growing commercial use of the Net is having the side effect of showing the actual cost of Net access, and despite the outcries of online activists and the magazine columnists who parrot the "free information" litany, the Internet has its costs.

For the individual without an organization behind her, though, the share of this cost is well within the range of average affordability. Anyone who can pay upwards of $40 for some mediocre cable TV system service (is there any other kind?) should have no trouble finding a Net access account within her means. Try substituting the Net for your cable for a month or two. You may never go back.

For those with more structured financial opportunities, community movements dedicated to making access available to the "have-nots" are spreading like a fungus. Even some libraries are allowing access on public terminals.

Computer Resources

The more computer you can afford the better, of course, but the basic text interactions on MUDs, and on Internet Relay Chat (IRC) can be achieved with comparatively little in the way of personal computer mule flesh. If your computer can run a terminal communication program and handle a modem, you are on your way. That would include just about every personal computer sold in the last ten years or more. But since the low-end home computer never seems to fall lower than $1,000, if you buy new it will probably cost you that much for a basic system. For that basic system these days, you are getting a lot more computer compared to even two years ago.

Go even cheaper by looking through the newspaper classified section for a used computer system. You may spot one for a few hundred dollars. If you've never seen any reason for having a computer before, you have one now—networking. But you don't have to spend a lot for a state-of-the-art system. Be sure to get the advice of a knowledgeable friend before buying a used computer, and always insist that the seller demonstrate the system before buying it.

As long as the machine can handle ASCII text and can support a modem and terminal software, MUDs are within striking range.

Modem

Modems (*modem* stands for MODulator/DEModulator) are the appliances that link a computer to a line through the normal phone jack. The *size* of a modem is measured by its speed in bits per second (bps). Bits per second is a measurement of how much bit-sized information your modem can process in any one second of time. There was a time when 2400 bps was a blazing speed. Now it's downright poky. But the price is right and a serviceable 2400 can be had for around $50. Here again, though, the low end is coming down. It soon may be difficult to find 2400s for sale.

Between Net lag and the reaction time of most MUD systems, a faster modem is not necessary for basic networking.

BBS

Electronic Bulletin Board Systems abound in every community. For the networking newcomer, this is the place to get your feet wet. A BBS is where you can find advice and knowledge about the bigger Net. And indeed, some community BBSs are connected to the Net. There are also smaller, self-sustaining networks run by associations of BBSs. These are called echo nets and mostly serve as a forum for messages that are transferred between systems once a night. Check with local computer user clubs for the numbers of BBSs near you. Look for a huge publication called *Computer Shopper* at a newsstand. It runs a list of BBSs every other week. Or consult the directory of a little book called *Free Electronic Networks* (Prima, ISBN 1-55958-415-7.)

Once you connect locally with a BBS, you may find it holds a repository of extremely reasonably-priced software, and perhaps it may even harbor a connection to the big Internet. A knowledgeable technical type—or three—will be around and about, and the BBS itself can serve as a gateway to interesting communication.

Communications or Terminal Software

The connections between your computer, modem, the phone lines, and an online service (whether it's a tiny BBS or a huge system like CompuServe) will be controlled on your end by your *communications*, sometimes called *terminal software*. All new modem or modem-equipped computer systems come bundled with adequate *comm* software. Normally you will find better software elsewhere, whether it's an expensive stand-alone product or shareware downloaded from an online source. Normally the shareware products are designed by folks with first-hand experience in day-to-day telecomputing (some terminal software seems to be designed by folks who have never fired up a modem under real-world telecomputing conditions). And the price is right.

Shareware

The software that can be acquired through BBSs is marketed using an innovation tailored for the medium. Shareware is software product that is set loose by its designers to be passed around from user to user to find its own market.

Terminal programs and other useful utilities can be downloaded to your own computer free, for evaluation. Then if you intend to use the software, you are honor-bound to pay for it after a period set by the maker. This allows the software maker to bypass the traditional retail market, with its expensive overhead and labor costs. Fully functional, professionally constructed software tools are available as shareware. Comparable products that might cost hundreds through "normal" commercial channels can often be found for $20 to $30.

Data Compression

Shareware programs come packaged in an archive—a single file that contains many other files—that has been compressed to save space. A popular compression product which is used to package shareware in this way is itself a shareware product. It's called PKZip. Archives that have been folded up using PKZip most often have a .zip extender. Some (like the PKZip distribution itself) may have an .exe extender. This is an executable file that will unravel itself. No decompression software is necessary. If you're going to be taking in a lot of software from online, you'll need to get a copy of PKZip to use its unzipping ability, and any other compression product that might be used by the BBS systems you call. (Other compression products include ARJ and LHA.)

Freeware

There are also software tools available for *no* cost at all. The designers made them and contributed to the world. An example is the UUENCODE/DECODE set of encryption tools. These are small programs that allow the exchange of large zipped or otherwise compressed or binary files through electronic mail.

Fear of Infection

Viruses are always a consideration. These destructive creations of remorseless techno-vandals must be constantly scanned for and eradicated. Make sure before going online that you have good weapons for the fight. Infection through reputable online services is rarer than some would have you believe. System operators (sysops) and network administrators (admins) are responsible for large monetary investments embodied in the computer systems they oversee. Some have paid for them out of their own pockets. You can be sure they take extreme measures to prevent infection. Often, though, you will see a disclaimer warning that the system does not scan for viruses.

Recommendation: be sure to acquire a scanner/cleaner that is updated regularly. Scan everything that comes into your computer whether by network transfer, by exchanging disks with others, or even commercially packaged products. There have been cases of commercial software and new blank disks serving as the medium for viral spread. Care should be taken, but fear of viruses is no reason to avoid going online.

Telephone Considerations

If you're not connecting through the Wide Area Network (WAN) of a large organization, you most likely will be accessing the Internet through your own telephone service, with modem and communications software.

Local, national and international services offer dial-up access to the Internet. If you have unlimited local telephone dialing, and the number is local, then the calls add no expense to your online sessions.

Commercial services, on the other hand, sometimes charge by the hour. Sometimes they charge at a flat rate. Often they cannot be reached by local dialing, but must be linked by using a PDN, or Public Data Network. SprintNet® is one such PDN, and depending on the service you are reaching, there may be an hourly surcharge that varies according to the time of day.

The telephone and networking landscape is always shifting and may vary greatly according to local conditions. Shop around for the best telephone access according to your own geography.

The following are some listings of service providers and Free-Nets. As mentioned before, scout out local bulletin boards for information. Check with local computer user groups. Ask at the library. Many libraries are intensely interested in networking. Someone at your local library may have information.

Technology

Though the approach of this book is more for some generic computer, the exploration of MUDs and the book's writing was all done with the most common technology available for the individual PC owner: the MS-DOS/Intel/IBM clone. The concepts apply to all other computer formats, though perhaps with different terminology. Macs do the same thing as Sun as Amiga as Intel-based as PowerPC. Differing terminology and chip differences notwithstanding, they all process text as bits and graphics (which are just huge, resource-devouring armies of bits). For the purposes of MUDding, just as online a person's age, race and gender are nearly always irrelevant, there are no differences between computers. This may also change. As more graphics-based MUDs come online, they will demand more resources and some destinations may offer graphical access only.

Free-Nets

Running on occasional donations and lots of volunteer dedication, the Free-Net phenomenon is gaining followers daily. The Free-Nets are continuing, on a larger scale, the idea of the community BBS, which started as the part-time work of committed enthusiasts. The concept is expanded and enhanced by Free-Nets offering full-scale community networking at an extremely low price (some demand a one-time registration fee of $10).

The National Public Telecomputing Network, which organizes this phenomenon, originated in research projects conducted in the mid-80s at Case Western Reserve University in Cleveland, Ohio.

Many major and not-so-major metropolitan areas now have Free-Nets. Many more are organizing.

Here is a list of operating Free-Net systems. Try logging in as "visitor" or "guest" to get a look around. (Sometimes the password will also be "guest" or "visitor," or just press ENTER.)

Remember, these systems are community-supported and donations keep them going.

Tempe, AZ
AzTeC Computing
602-965-5985 (voice)
602-965-4151 (modem)
telnet: aztec.asu.edu

Los Angeles, CA
Los Angeles Free-Net
818-954-0080 (voice)
818-776-5000 (modem)
telnet: lafn.org

Denver, CO
Denver Free-Net—Denver
303-270-4300 (voice)
303-270-4865 (modem)
telnet: free-net.hsc.colorado.edu

Broward County, FL
SEFLIN Free-Net
305-357-7318 (voice)
305-765-4332 (modem)
telnet: bcfree-net.seflin.lib.fl.us

Tallahassee, FK
Tallahassee Free-Net
904-644-1796 (voice)
904-488-5056 (modem)
telnet: free-net.fsu.edu

Champaign-Urbana, IL
Prairienet
217-244-3299 (voice)
217-255-9000 (modem)
telnet: prairienet.org

Almont, MI
Almont Expression
810-798-8150 (voice)
810-798-8290 (modem)

Battle Creek, MI
Great Lakes Free-Net
616-961-4166 (voice)
616-969-4536 (modem)

Detroit, MI

Greater Detroit Free-Net
313-825-5293 (voice)
No dial-up access.
telnet: detroit.free-net.org

Columbia, MO

Columbia Online Information
Network (COIN)
314-443-3161, ext. 350 (voice)
314-884-7000 (modem)
telnet: bigcat.missouri.edu

Springfield, MO

ORION
417-837-5050, ext. 15 (voice)
417-864-6100 (modem)
telnet: ozarks.sgcl.lib.mo.us

Dillon, MT

Big Sky Telegraph
406-683-7338 (voice)
406-683-7680 (modem)
telnet: 192.231.192.1

Buffalo, NY

Buffalo Free-Net
716-877-8800 ext. 451 (voice)
716-645-3085 (modem)
telnet: free-net.buffalo.edu
Visitor login: freeport

Cincinnati, OH

Tristate Online
606-781-5575 (modem)
telnet: tso.uc.edu

Cleveland, OH

Cleveland Free-Net
216-368-2982 (voice)
216-368-3888 (modem)
telnet: free-net-in-a.cwru.edu

Columbus, OH

Greater Columbus Free-Net
614-292-4132 (voice)
614-292-7501 (modem)
telnet: free-net.columbus.oh.us

Dayton, OH

Dayton Free-Net
513-873-4035 (voice)
513-229-4373 (modem)
telnet: 130.108.128.174

Elyria, OH

Lorain County Free-Net
800-227-7113 ext. 2451 (voice)
216-277-2451 (voice)
216-366-9721 (voice)
telnet: free-net.lorain.oberlin.edu

Medina, OH

Medina County Free-Net
216-725-1000 ext. 2550 (voice)
216-723-6732 (modem)

Youngstown, OH

Youngstown Free-Net
216-742-3075 (voice)
216-742-3072 (modem)
telnet: yfn2.ysu.edu

Providence, RI

Ocean State Free-Net

401-277-2726 (voice)

401-831-4640 (voice)

telnet: 192.207.24.10

El Paso, TX

Rio Grande Free-Net

915-775-6077 (voice)

915-775-5600 (voice)

telnet: rgfn.epcc.edu

Richmond, VA

Ccentral Virginia's Free-Net

804-828-6650 (voice)

No dial-up access.

telnet: free-net.vcu.edu

Seattle, WA

Seattle Community Network

206-865-3424 (voice)

206-386-4140 (modem)

telnet: scn.org

Tri-Cities, WA

Free-Net —Tri-Cities

509-586-6481 (voice)

509-375-1111 (modem)

Trail, BC

CIAO! Free-Net

604-368-2233 (voice)

604-368-5764 (modem)

telnet: 142.231.5.1

Victoria, BC

Victoria Free-Net

604-385-4302 (voice)

604-595-2300 (modem)

telnet: free-net.victoria.bc.ca

Ottawa, ON

National Capital Free-Net

613-788-2600 ext. 3701 (voice)

613-564-3600 (modem)

telnet: free-net.carleton.ca

Erlangen, Germany

Free-Net Erlangen-Nuernburg

49-9131-85-4735 (voice)

49-9131-85-8111 (modem)

telnet: 131.188.192.11

Visitor login: gast

Wellington, New Zealand

Wellington Citynet

64-4-801-3303 (voice)

64-4-801-3060 (modem)

telnet: kosmos.wcc.govt.nz

Public Dial-Up

Below are listed some services that offer Internet access, some more commercial (pricier) than others. Many of these services also function as "wholesale" access points for other services. Call for information and access details for the individual.

You'll pay a premium, per-hour charge for 800 toll-free services. Some can be accessed by the public data networks (PDN), which have local numbers nearly everywhere. Surcharges for PDNs and 800 numbers vary. If a service is in your local area code, start there. A few have dial-up points of presence (POPs) in and around particular regions. Listed below are the name and reach of the service, and a voice telephone number to call for information.

To reach a service by PDN, first you must make contact and get instructions for logging on. The service will have a list of phone numbers, from which you choose the one closest to you.

Scoping

Scoping is a little-known telephone company feature that allows you to extend your local calling area into nearby and adjacent exchanges for a small monthly fee. Just in case some of the access numbers you come across here are close, but not close enough, call up your local phone company customer service number and say, "I want to scope to..." and give them the exchange. They will explain all your options.

a2i communications
Area codes 408, 415
408-293-8078 (voice)

Tundra Services
Area code 907
907-465-6453 (voice)

Anomaly
Area codes 401, 508
401-273-4669 (voice)

Ariadne
Area code 301—Athens, Greece
301 65-13-392 (voice)

The Black Box
Area code 713
713-480-2684 (voice)

Communications Accessibles Montreal
Area code 514
514-931-0749 (voice)

CAPCON Library Network
Area code 202, 301, 410, 703
202-331-5771 (voice)

E & S Systems Public Access
Area codes 619
619-278-4641 (voice)

Cooperative Library Agency for Systems and Services
Area codes 310, 415, 510, 619, 714, 818, 800
800-488-4559 (voice)

Community News Service
Area codes 303, 719, 800
719-592-1240 (voice)

Concert-Connect
Area codes 704, 910, 919
919-248-1999 (voice)

connect.com.au pty ltd
Area codes 61 3, 61 2 (Australia)
61 3 5282239 (voice)

CTS Network Services
Area code 619
619-637-3637 (voice)

CR Laboratories Dialup Internet Access
Area codes 213, 310, 404, 415, 510, 602, 707, 800
415-381-2800 (voice)

Colorado Supernet, Inc.
Area codes 303, 719, 800
303-273-3471 (voice)

Data Basix
Area code 602
602-721-1988 (voice)

Demon Internet Systems
Area code 44 (0)81
(London, England)
44 (0)81 349 0063 (voice)

DELPHI
Area codes 617, PDN
800-544-4005 (voice)

DIAL n' CERF
Area codes 213, 310, 415, 510, 619, 714, 818, 800
800-876-2373 (voice)
619-455-3900

The Direct Connection
Area code 44 (0)81
(London, England)
44 (0)81 317 0100 (voice)

Echo Communications
Area code 212
212-255-3839 (voice)

Eskimo North
Area code 206
206-367-7457 (voice)

Evergreen Communications
Area code 602
602-955-8315 (voice)

Express Access—A service of Digital Express Group
Area codes 202, 301, 410, 703, 714, 908
800-969-9090 (voice)
301-220-2020 (voice)

Freelance Systems Programming
Area codes 513
513-254-7246 (voice)

CyberGate, Inc.
Area codes 305, 407
305-428-GATE (voice)

Halcyon
Area code 206
206-955-1050 (voice)

Holonet
Area codes 510, PDN
510-704-0160 (voice)

HookUp Communication Corporation
Area Codes 416, 519, 800, PDN
(Ontario, Canada)
519-747-4110 (voice)

UK PC User Group
Area codes 44 (0)81 (London, England)
44 (0)81 863 6 646 (voice)

The IDS World Network
Area code 401
401-884-7856 (voice)

IEunet Ltd.
Area code 353 1 (Dublin, Ireland)
353 1 6790832 (voice)

Institute for Global Communications
Area codes 415, 800, PDN
415-442-0220 (voice)

Internet Direct, Inc.
Area code 602
602-274-0100 (voice)
602-324-0100 (voice)

INS—Inter Networking Systems
49 2305 356505 (voice)

InterAccess
Area codes 708, 312, 815
800-967-1580 (voice)

The John von Neumann Computer Network
Area codes 201, 203, 215, 401, 516, 609, 908, 800
800-35-TIGER (voice)
609-897-7300 (voice)

KAIWAN Public Access Internet Online Services
Area codes 213, 310, 714
714-638-2139 (voice)

Maestro
Area codes 212, 718
212-240-9600 (voice)

MCSnet

Area codes 312, 708, 815

312-248-UNIX (voice)

Texas Metronet

Area codes 214, 817

214-705-2900 (voice)

817-543-8756 (voice)

Merit Network, Inc.

Area codes 202, 301, 313, 517, 616, 703, 810, 906, PDN

313-764-9430 (voice)

Millennium Online

Area code PDN

800-736-0122 (voice)

MindVOX

Area codes 212, 718

212-989-2418 (voice)

MSen

Area codes 313, 810

313-998-4562 (voice)

MV Communications, Inc.

Area code 603

603-429-2223 (voice)

NEARnet

Area codes 508, 603, 617

617-873-8730 (voice)

netcom Online Communication Services

Area codes 206, 213, 214, 303, 310, 312, 404, 408, 415, 503, 510, 617, 619, 703, 714, 718, 818, 916

408-554-8649 (voice)

800-501-8649 (voice)

North Shore Access

Area codes 617, 508

617-593-3110 (voice)

NovaLink

Area codes 508, 617, PDN

800-274-2814 (voice)

Nuance Network Services

Area code 205

205-533-4296 (voice)

South Coast Computing Services, Inc.

Area code 713

713-661-3301 (voice)

Northwest Nexus Inc.

Area code 206

206-455-3505 (voice)

OARnet

Area codes 614, 513, 419, 216, 800

614-292-8100 (voice)

Old Colorado City Communications

Area code 719

719-632-4848 (voice)

719-593-7575 (voice)

719-636-2040 (voice)

Olympus

Area code 206

206-385-0464 (voice)

PANIX Public Access Unix

Area codes 212, 718

212-877-4854 (voice)

212-691-1526 (voice)

The Pipeline

Area codes 212, 718, PDN

212-267-3636 (voice)

The Portal System

Area codes 408, 415, PDN

408-973-9111 (voice)

PREPnet

Area codes 215, 412, 717, 814

412-268-7870 (voice)

PSILink

Area code PDN

703-620-6651 (voice)

PSI's World-Dial Service

Area code PDN

703-620-6651 (voice)

PUCnet Computer Connections

Area code 403

403-448-1901 (voice)

Systems Solutions

Area code 302

302-378-1386 (voice)

800-331-1386 (voice)

Sugar Land Unix

Area codes 504, 713

713-438-4964 (voice)

Teleport

Area code 503

503-223-4245 (voice)

Telerama Public Access Internet

Area code 412

412-481-3505 (voice)

The Meta Network

Area codes 703, 202, 301, PDN

703-243-6622 (voice)

UUNET Canada, Inc.

Area codes 403, 416, 514, 519, 604, 613, 905

416-368-6621 (voice)

UUnorth

Area codes 416, 519, 613

416-225-8649 (voice)

Vnet Internet Access, Inc.

Area codes 704, 919

704-374-0779 (voice)

The Whole Earth 'Lectronic Link (The Well)

Area codes 415, PDN

415-332-4335 (voice)

APK

Area code 216

216-481-9428 (voice)

The World

Area codes 617, PDN

617-739-0202 (voice)

Wyvern Technologies, Inc.

Area code 804

804-622-4289 (voice)

Xnet Information Systems

Area codes 312, 708, 815

708 983-6064 (voice)

Getting It On

The features and functions of online life are many and varied. Besides connecting remotely with another computer far away—the online activity that computers seem to have been made for all along—the transfer of many different kinds of data awaits you when you score a network account.

For the purposes of this book , *net* is the target function of your quest for access. The online services that surround this key remote computing function are as many and varied as their management, and with the diversity of systems available, there are some for every taste (although every service is not available in every area). You may be surprised—after a lifetime of dealing with a monolithic US phone system—at how many individual personalities these services show to the public.

The following four system profiles can give an idea of what's available from smallest to largest, with a pair of in-betweens.

Jersey Devil

Starting small, here's an example of a community BBS run by one of those aforementioned devoted enthusiasts. There may be a similar system near you. Ask around about something like Jersey Devil.

Vince Quaresima is the sysop of this BBS, located in Browns Mills, New Jersey. "Online continuously since January 15, 1984," says Vince Q, as he's known in the active South Jersey BBS community. Is that a record for longest continual up-time for an independent BBS in the state? "In the country," he's quick to interject.

Quaresima develops software, teaches high school and is planning a 1995 run for state office. Jersey Devil is a prime example of a systems operator who will get his board on the Net by hook, crook or packet radio. And that's just how it's done here. For more than a year, Jersey Devil has been offering Internet access to the caller on its single incoming phone line. The connection to the Internet is achieved by ham radio.

The opening greeter screen of Jersey Devil BBS, linked to the Internet by the two-meter ham radio band.

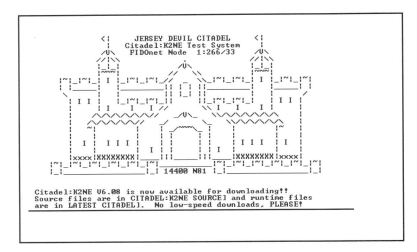

Using a radio modem with a high speed of 1200 bps, a call through the system can be a halting process. "It can get pretty laggy," Quaresima says. Lag is the term for delays caused by network deficiencies or overcrowding. Some causes of lag are more close to home than others. Other than annoying delays in conversations—at times reminding one of the time lag between questions and answers on those old NASA moon missions—the lag is rarely intolerable.

Radio waves can carry data packets like any wired form of transmission. The Jersey Devil BBS link uses a transponder hub operated by the Camden-Burlington Packet Radio Association. There may, at times, be 100 radio onliners using the hub. Such traffic can cause long delays. The 23 or so users who use accounts at JD may not do much complaining, though. Their access is free. The agreement by which the association gets its link precludes any BBS downlink from re-selling access. Quaresima says he has never charged for accounts, even before Internet access, and has never, as is common practice in homegrown BBSdom, made any plea for donations.

Whatever its past, and however lagged, present plans have JD moving nicely into the future, well, the near future anyway. "We'll have a land-line to the Internet soon," says Vince Q. He plans to charge because he'll have to, and because this may be his small window of opportunity to turn a decade's worth of dedication into a little extra cash. "It'll all be over in three years," he says, "when the phone company gets into it."

For now though, when the land line comes in, the projected price will be $15 to $20 per month for a full access account, with special rates for students in the summer.

The modem number for Jersey Devil is 609-893-2152.

PICS Online!

The next step up is a system that also started as a small community BBS but grew into a more or less local online service for western Camden County, NJ. PICS Online! has over a dozen phone lines. The system runs on 20 computers in two different locations. It's an example of a BBS that has graduated from hobby to sideline to full-scale business. PICS' sysop, Terry Rossi, also maintains a demanding full-time job as a supervisor of technical support for a company that makes manufacturing software.

PICS has made a gradual run up into full Internet service provider. Two years ago, Rossi began to offer e-mail service and access to a few hundred of the wide-open Usenet "newsgroups"—the chattering, and sometimes raunchy, electronic conferencing message channels that ride the Internet data paths. "Now PICS users can reach out into the depth and breadth of the global Internet," says Rossi. Telnet, FTP and the World Wide Web are now available for connecting PICS users to the world in real-time.

Besides the Internet gateway, PICS still retains the features that has made it a community BBS, with thousands of files of all types available for downloading—no FTP necessary.

From the PICS Intergate screen, users can FTP, Telnet to a MUD or choose from a list of sites for linking. There are many small to medium independent services like PICS cropping up.

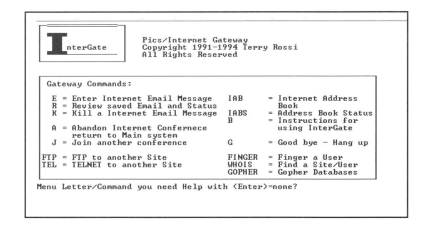

Also available are many of the network messaging conferences from the largest of the echo nets (a form of do-it-yourself networking that exchanges messages nightly), Fidonet.

PICS patron members get one hour per day online at these prices: $25 per month; $45 for three months; $120 for 12 months. (Non-members get the same price for access, but are only online for 30 minutes per day.)

A PICS Patron membership can be had at the following rates: $10 for one month; $35 for three months; $55 for 12 months. Call 609-753-2540 by modem to reach PICS.

Pipeline

If you don't live near either one of the above systems, you can use the SprintNet PDN to reach Pipeline. The centerpiece of Pipeline access is the software tool that members can use as a front-end. The program is a GUI—graphical user interface—that comes in a Windows and Macintosh version.

Built into the attractive screens are commands for navigating around the system. The user need do nothing except point and click at the desired item or activity. Among the many features are the usual array of Internet commands: FTP, Telnet, gopher, archie and access to any of the thousands of Usenet newsgroups. There is also an access to the Lynx browser, another program that serves as the navigation tool for the World Wide Web. WWW is the hypertext search system that is finding wide acceptance as more information providers make their output available in the HyperText Markup Language (HTML) format. Lynx provides its own menu of easy jumps to gophers, files, Telnet servers and everything else, and it's plugged right into Pipeline.

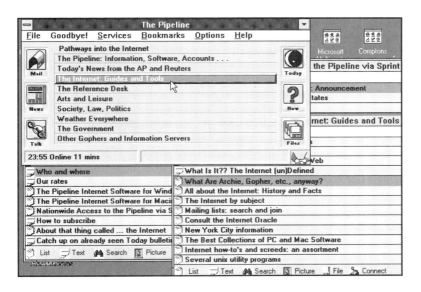

The user can have many windows open at once, while the Pipeline GUI sends and receives data at the same time, choosing from the full complement of Internet features.

Except for a few minor kinks to be worked out, the Pipeline software is a wonder. It represents all the ease-of-use that the new interfaces are meant to provide.

The software can be downloaded for free. It includes a built-in facility for finding the SprintNet dial-up POP number nearest you. Once you get the software, just choose Connect! from the menu bar and the software will instruct you as to what to so next.

To get the software by modem, call: 212-267-6432 (high speed) or 212-267-7341. Log in as a guest.

The basic account on Pipeline is $20 per month, with a connect time charge of $2 per hour. Other special plans include: The TIW (Toe in the Water) Plan: $15 per month, which includes five free hours; The 20/20 Plan: $20 per monthly, which includes 20 free hours; The IIMO (Internet Is My Oyster) Plan: $35 for unlimited time.

As a kind of bulk rate deal, users who can pay for 10 months in advance get 12 months credit, but may, nevertheless, cancel at any time and receive a refund for their remaining time. Pipeline's voice number is 212-267-3636.

Delphi Internet

The biggest nationwide service that offers full Internet access is Delphi Internet. An elaborate electronic community in its own right, Delphi Internet led the way for large-system commercial Internet access. Many others, like America Online, followed suit with Internet e-mail and some other limited features, but, at this writing, Delphi Internet is still the only major online service with telnet. (Though Prodigy recently announced a service and may have instituted full access by the time this book reaches market.)

Fully text-based, Delphi Internet may seem a bit old-fashioned, but the loyal users provide a lively meeting place, with discussion forums on hundreds of subjects, online games and, of course, Internet access to all the network sites there are.

Delphi Internet has recently released a graphical front-end for access, but reps there are careful not to have it labeled a "GUI." It is being call an "interactive navigation tool" that provides automatic log-ons via direct dial or PDN. Though it is graphical, it does not provide icon-style point and click interaction throughout. In other words, you can tell Internav to take you to the Internet forum or other areas on Delphi Internet by pointing the mouse to a rectangular button at the top of the screen, but once you get there, it's necessary to type in text commands as before.

Internav has an attractive screen presence, though, and provides an editor for composing mail messages, which beats using the online editor hands down.

Internav had a quiet release and though it is not being called a "beta" version, was still in its late development stage at the time of this writing. It is available for MS-DOS computers only, running on a 386 processor or better, with 4 megabytes of RAM and Windows 3.1. Download Internav from the "Using Delphi" forum area of the main menu.

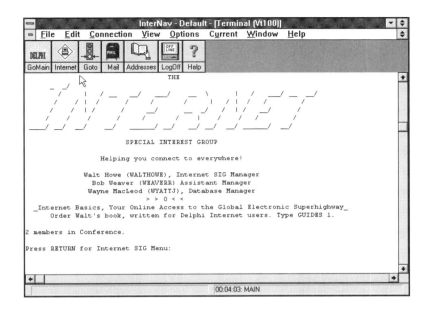

Delphi Internet is available nearly everywhere, has been offering full-time Internet access longer than any major commercial service, and has a helpful staff of netheads to lend a hand.

The Delphi Internet link works like a charm and has a database full of helpful files, a utilities menu with features like ping, netfind, whois, gopher and archie. The Usenet area has many of the more popular groups and a facility for finding those informational files known as FAQs (Frequently Asked Questions files). Mostly these FAQ files deal with newsgroup topics, so that new folks do not subject themselves to tongue-lashings from touchy discussion area trolls if they happen to repeat a question that has been discussed at some point in the past.

Delphi Internet can be reached by PDN or by the local number in Boston. There is no PDN surcharge in off-peak hours, making Delphi Internet access one of the more economical offerings around.

There are two payment plans: The 10/4 plan gets four hours of time per month for $10. The 20/20 Advantage plan is 20 hours for $20. Hours spent online over the plan maximums are billed at the rate of $1.80 per hour. There is a monthly $3 surcharge for the Internet access. Delphi Internet offers a free trial five hours of access. Voice numbers are 800-695-4005 and 617-491-3393.

SprintNet Access

From outside of New York (Pipeline's base) and Boston (Delphi Internet's home) access is available from thousands of US and hundreds of overseas localities through the SprintNet data network. The local numbers can also be had from SprintNet (800-877-5045). For Pipeline, the surcharge for connecting through SprintNet is $5 per hour during peak periods (8 AM - 5 PM Monday - Friday, Eastern standard time) and $2.50 an hour evenings, weekends, and holidays.

On Delphi Internet, accessing (through SprintNet, or through another available PDN, Tymnet) is charged at the rate of $9.50 per hour during peak business hours. There is no charge in off-peak and weekend hours.

Launch Yourself

Now, if you don't have access already, it shouldn't be too hard to get some. Fiddle around with the commands and read all the help files you can get your hands on, then come back here when you're ready to MUD.

Oh, and before venturing further, where might one find that talking tree? Well, it's at MediaMoo, and we may just see it again before this book is through.

Chapter 2

How Did We Get MUD?

the origin of these interactive environments—the MUDs in all their flavors and the worldwide chat channels of IRC—can be found in an obscure demonstration of a pioneer computing machine which took place in 1940. George R. Stibitz had made the trip to a mathematics conference. Rather than lug the big machine he had invented for calculating with him, he left it at his office. Stibitz then linked up by telegraph to perform complex calculations—computing over the distance between New York and Dartmouth College in Hanover, New Hampshire by telegraph—the natural thing to do. To Stibitz, using the primeval "server" from a distance was not worthy of comment. The mathematicians, on hearing solutions to problems that the best of them couldn't have done nearly as fast, were suitably dazzled.

With this reference to the telegraph, then, one might look even farther back to peg the beginnings of all this to Samuel F. P. Morse—not Alexander G. Bell, as most commentators seem to do. Morse invented electronic communications; his dot-or-dash code was a binary one. If anything then, what Bell did with analog audio telephony could be regarded as a delaying sidetrack on the road to complete digital telecomputing. We're back on track now.

Most books on networking fail to mention the next big step in the process—the SAGE system of air warning radar picket defenses, built in the 1950s to guard against an over-the-pole Soviet bomber attack.

Networking's life is often said to have begun in academia, with the military contribution and the impetus of foreign threat relegated to little more than a footnote, if referred to at all.

DragonSpires: A Glimpse of the Future

Currently under construction is what may be the model for the interactive multi-user dimension of the future. *DragonSpires,* a graphical, Internetted, multi-user system, is a work-in-progress (but is quickly gathering serious backers, according to the designer). It moves far beyond mere text room-and-action descriptions. You can *see* what happens to your armor-plated avatar in colorful, graphic detail, and all the other folks who have logged on are represented by animated figures, as well.

At the time of this writing, version 1.5 of the *DragonSpires* system was about to give way to 1.6. Players could choose the colors of their armor, shields and plumes; they could also pick up objects and conduct duels in an arena set aside for voluntary swordplay. Sound card support had also been added, with background music and a few sound effects. For instance, when the player happens upon a dog bone, picks it up, and suddenly finds he has *become* the dog, the command for "swinging sword" then makes the dog bark. The yapping comes through your sound card speakers. The designer, Dr. Cat —a veteran game designer with many commercial credits (including work on two parts of the Ultima series)—hints that there may be human speech transfer supported in some future version.

The *DragonSpires* client program, the part that computes and reproduces the nice graphics on your home computer, runs on MS-DOS systems only. The MUD cannot be accessed without it. At this point, the package includes a simple communications driver, through which the dial-up connection can be made. The player then uses regular telnet to connect to the MUD. It will also connect through a shell account and telnet at a UNIX-based service provider. Get the client by FTP at **ftp.eden.com** in the **/pub/dspire** directory. The latest version of the archive will be named something like **dspire*.zip**.

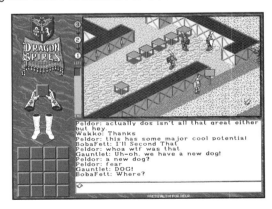

In the DragonSpires MUD environment, you can see your online presence depicted graphically.

It was in this military project, though, that the first large-scale networking occurred (it would now be called a WAN, Wide Area Network). First demonstrated in 1953, SAGE had input devices (radar towers) and output devices (display screens) sharing data transmitted over a distance. To save U.S. taxpayer money, and to cut the development time dramatically, the regular North American civilian telephone net—already in place—was used to link the command centers with the towers.

For this crash program, the experts came up with the simple device, called a modem, that translates bits into sound. (And with all the recent hullabaloo about computers merging with telephones lately, if you don't know what a modem is, you may not really want to be reading this book. But just for completeness' sake: a modem performs the transactions that make computer information into telephone-readable sound information.) SAGE is also notable because it saw the use of the first random access memory (RAM) and saw the initiating of some key time-sharing programming techniques.

Time sharing was the next computing development to take hold, in the 1960s, and it found its place in both business and academia. More suitably described as time-slicing, the distribution of the computer resources among users made the most of the fast integrated circuits that were being introduced by arranging for the computer to do many things at once. The machines have no trouble remembering many tasks and made use of every bit of time between the interminable split seconds it takes a human to type in keystrokes.

Schools of higher learning set their students on a course for designing the next wave of computer usage pattern, the multiple-user network. Elizabeth Reid, in her Master's thesis, (English, University of Melbourne) describes how MIT "in a cost-saving move set...students to designing their own multi-user operating system. ...there needed to be more than one set of input and output devices connected to the computer. From each of these multiple terminals, different users could share the same computer resources. The system that they designed, and named the Incompatible Timesharing System, was one of the first of this new breed of operating systems. ITS and other systems like it quickly supplanted the old single-user systems."

Dartmouth was another school that came up with a time sharing system, which was used to make computer resources widely available to business and research interests.

And on the Eighth Day...UNIX

Or so it would seem—if you asked the scads of techies who eat, sleep, live and die by the archaic dictates of the ancient multi-user operating system family. No system has managed to replace UNIX, and no one in the name of all that is Microsoft can foresee anything replacing it in the near future, though it is ripe for the picking.

The operating system has been around since 1969, over 25 years. In a business where generations of improvements are happening in timeframes measured in months, this would qualify as venerable to say the least. But as the magazine writers love to say, UNIX is a "robust" system, and built for multiple users. Its name is rooted in the word "united" because UNIX can be networked among otherwise incompatible computer systems. In UNIX was the birth of interoperability, a pan-platform way of computing that is only now taking hold in the business world, where devotion to a monolithic system made (and sometimes *operated*) by a single company was the norm.

UNIX has such a strong hold on its adherents that many regard users of other systems as a lower form of life. Anything that proves to be so useful will have its fanatics.

At around the same time, during those fabled late 60s, the U.S. government, again in reaction to an airborne threat—this time in the form of Communist nuclear-tipped ICBMs—embarked on a mission, undertaken by military and research computer wizards, to set up a type of distributed networking that would not be vulnerable if one or many of its *nodes* were taken out by nukes. The resulting technique was called *packet switching*. The data, whether it be the text of an e-mail message, or the continuous ebb and flow of a "real-time" connection, was split into small discrete packets which were free to find their own paths to the destination through an address that each packet carries with it. The addressing scheme and the suite of commands that executed it eventually came to be known as the Transmission Control Protocol/Internet Protocol (TCP/IP).

This combination of UNIX and TCP/IP came to be the predominant networking/operating system used, but it is not the only scheme. Other operating systems can run TCP/IP, like DOS and VMS, and so they too can communicate with any other TCP/IP installation, no matter what the operating platform. Only those systems using TCP/IP, though, can be accessed through what has come to be known as "The Internet."

Online Life

Toward the late 70s and early 80s, commercial user networks began to appear. CompuServe, and others like it, offered news and discussion areas for individuals not fortunate enough to have fallen into the academic research computing environment. For a fee, a user could link up with others from all over the world.

Concurrently, independent networks began sprouting up. Self-sustaining online entities known as Bulletin Board Systems, in many shapes, sizes and compatibilities, began to organize into networks. These are known as *echo* networks, since without the excess of resources granted to universities by virtue of military projects, they could not maintain full-time devoted connections, but would link up once per night, relaying messages and program files along the chain of BBSs. Thus, a message might take a day or so to reach its destination, repeating along the link like an echo.

Many of the users, both in academia and independent, having an affinity for the technology, and an affinity for science fiction and fantasy, commenced to apply their outside leisure interests to their networking endeavors.

The Lure of Role-Playing

With the advent of networked environments came experimentation with the language of single user interaction. On research computers around the world were the first glimmerings of serious computer resources being turned to leisure: role-playing activities.

According to Reid:

> The computer aficionados at the Stanford Artificial Intelligence Laboratory of the early 1970s were well-known for being fantasy fans. Rooms in the AI Lab were named after locations described in J.R.R. Tolkien's *Lord of the Rings*, and the printer in the lab was rigged so that it could print in three different Elven fonts. It was one of these fantasy fans who wrote the first virtual reality computer game. Donald Woods, a veteran of MIT's Spacewar, discovered a quite different kind of game being run on a computer at the Xerox Corporation's Palo Alto Research Center. The program depicted an explorer seeking treasure in a network of caverns. It was an entirely text-based game. There were no spaceships to be shot, no graphics at all, just descriptions of localities and prompts asking players where they wished to go or what they wanted to do next. Woods was entranced by the game. He contacted the programmer, Will Crowther, talked to him about it, and decided to expand Crowther's program into a more complex adventure game. What he wrote was ADVENT, more commonly referred to as Adventure, in which a player assumes the role of a traveler in a Tolkienesque setting, fighting off enemies, overcoming obstacles through clever tricks, and eventually discovering treasure.
>
> Adventure players were presented with text describing scenes...

From this, in the early 80s, emerged a short heyday for text adventures like the ZORK series. A company called Infocom had a run of game successes using puzzles and quests in a computer-mediated text environment. As computer graphics improved, these text-only genres fell by the wayside. But there is still a devoted following for them and an active cadre of creators who write text adventures. They are written with programming systems called ADL, Adventure Definition Languages. Discussion of them can be found in the USENET newsgroups (See chapter 3) devoted to *interactive fiction*.

Text adventures and scenes, and eventually multiple-user involvement in them, would combine in the form of the first MUD. Put together by a group of programmers at Essex University in the United Kingdom, MUD stood for Multi-User Dungeon (later the D would be de-gamed and attached to the more dignified *Dimension* or *Domain*).

And so MUD comes down to us. One of inventors, Richard Bartle, has been running a MUD commercially since the early 80s. Roy Trubshaw, the original programmer, recently re-united with Bartle in the venture, which is making a go of commercial MUD-providing. Who better to tell the origins of MUD than someone who was there:

The Story of the Birth of MUDs as related by Richard Bartle

Roy [Trubshaw] is always somewhat bemused by the success of MUD, and the fact that all these people want to play such games. He's a damned fine programmer, though! The first version was written in 1978 by Roy Trubshaw, with helpful programming suggestions by Keith Rautenbach and others, and help/praise from Nigel Roberts and Richard Bartle (me). It was not designed as a game at this point; it was mainly a test to see whether Roy's ideas for using shared memory to implement the system would work. They did. The program was written in MACRO-10 on a DEC system-10 mainframe at Essex University in the UK. I still have a printout of this program ("I am the genie of the watering can"). The main comment calls it "MUDD - Multi-User game of Adventurous Endeavour," but the two Ds are a typo; the game was always called MUD. That D, incidentally, is not because the game was set in a dungeon; rather, it was named that way because at the time there was no generic "Adventure game" concept, and there were only two such games in common currency: ADVENTURE and ZORK. ADVENTURE was known as ADVENT (DEC-10s had six-character filenames) and ZORK was known as DUNGEN (which was a Fortran rewrite of the original version in MDL).

Since Roy's program was to be a multi-user game of the type typified by ADVENT and DUNGEN, he thought the name ought to reflect that fact, so the "Dungeon" part refers to DUNGEN. That's the story, anyway; personally, I think Roy just liked the acronym MUD and then looked around for something the D could stand for!

The second version was written entirely by Roy, also in MACRO-10 assembler, in late 1978. The acronym was "Multiple User Dungeon" in the source code here, but we always called it "multi-" rather than "multiple," and formalized that for version 3. Version 2 would be recognizable to today's players as a MUD. Roy saw the game architecture as consisting of two parts, the interpreter and the database. The database defined the game world, and the interpreter implemented it; in this sense, the database can be regarded as a programming language, and Roy named it MUDDL (Multi-User Dungeon Definition Language). "Muddle," incidentally, is how the ZORK programmers pronounced the name of the language they wrote ZORK in, MDL—a neat coincidence! This version of MUD was totally programmable by the players (or rather those for whom Roy turned on the appropriate privilege bit). Not only were rooms and objects programmable, but even commands were, and the database could be written out at any time

(continues)

(continued)

so that once a definition had been tested, it could be made permanent. Nigel and I chipped in with more suggestions, and created rooms/objects for the game (some of which survive in MUD2 to this day).

Programmability was not a great success. Too much precious memory was used up storing the code to parse the database (these were the days when we had 35K of 36-bit words to play with), and people kept adding things which were not in character with the rest of the game—or which downright contradicted it. Quality went right out the door, consistency was erratic, and most computer undergraduates can't spell. Also, the actual code of the interpreter was getting hard to maintain, machine code not being all that easy to chop around (especially when you only have line editors available). Roy, therefore, made the decision to rewrite the game from scratch, taking out the database parser and running it separately. The result was version 3 of MUD, now more commonly known as MUD1.

MUD1 used a revised version of MUDDL, incorporating some of the features of the ADVENT database. The database definition file was parsed by a program called DBASE (this was before the commercial product also called dBase was released), and the compiled result was dropped as a binary dump file. The architecture of the DEC-10 was such that this could be read in by the MUD interpreter, then saved in situ as an executable file; thus, all the initialization had been done and saved immediately, so there was no need to reread the database every time the game started (only when it had been changed).

The interpreter was asynchronous: when people ran the game, they all executed the interpreter itself, which has a shareable, writeable segment of memory which the various processes all accessed. A system of semaphores gave processes single-user access to individual sections of the segment for when they were making changes, but no semaphores locked all of the memory. Thus, if one player was executing a very long command (e.g. WHERE ALL), the interpreter would lock each room's content list in order, print out the contents, then go on to the next. Time-sharing saw to it that the other players didn't notice any delay. (A synchronous approach would be one in which each command is executed in its entirety before any other command is executed, which means that a lot more complicated things can be done, but a long command means everyone has to wait for it to terminate before their own commands execute.)

MUDDL was fast. Because it was tabular, a command was executed by looking it up in a table, then finding a match for the object and instrument given by the user. However, its complexity was not great, due to the asynchronous nature of the database. As it was, anomalies could happen. Worse though, recursion and looping weren't written into MUDDL, and the granularity of its commands was too high (it had a built-in version of the KILL command, for example, which was explicitly oriented to a fantasy role-playing milieu). That said, MUDDL was easy to use, and several databases were written for it by other people, the most successful of

(continues)

(continued)

which, MIST, is still something of a legend among its former players, even today.

In 1984/85, I rewrote MUD completely, the result of which is now known as MUD2. MUD2 uses a synchronous architecture, made possible by the fact that computers now run a lot faster than they did in the days of MUD1. Its programming language, MUDDLE, is a complete language in itself, looking a little like an object-oriented flavor of Prolog, but explicitly meant for writing MUDs. It is, however, powerful enough to use for other things.

[Excerpted from e-mail correspondence with the author.]

MUD-O-RAMA

And now there are hundreds of MUDs running on the Internet and off, including some under the direction of the originators. "In the UK, we have one dial-up (system) only," says Bartle, meaning the user would modem to the site over the phone line, "which has been running for four years or so, and two others that are on the Internet. One of these, Sonet, is, however, primarily for dial-up users. They're attached to a cable phone network which gives local calls for free after 7 p.m., something completely unheard of in the UK! Although people can play Sonet over the Internet, it's geared to dial-up users."

The fee is about $2 per hour, says Bartle. "Of this, the networks take the lion's share (and the lioness', and all the cubs), but it still makes enough for me not to have to go out and get a proper job."

Richard Bartle: Prime Mover of MUDs (circa mid-1980's version).

Social MUDding

Though MUDs that have grown from the Trubshaw/Bartle model evolved into many flavors of fantasy and adventure themes, the techniques have more recently been devoted to those online denizens who like to gather—perhaps role-play a bit, but mostly just gather—and chat in surroundings where, though you may find a sword or two, there is no possibility of a hack or a slash.

James Aspnes (now at Yale), while a member of the faculty of Carnegie-Mellon University, took the idea of multiple-user environments and turned it to the creation of more sociable textual metaphors. Social MUDs have little or no goals to achieve, other than the participation of the players in building and shaping their own environments. Once versed in the programming languages of such MUDS (and MOOs, which are MUD Objected-Oriented, a particular style of programming theory put into practice), a proficient player can build surroundings that, in the least, are personally gratifying, and at the outside may be intriguing to anyone who happens by.

The Birth of Tinymud as related by James Aspnes.

The story of TinyMUD basically goes like this. I'd known about previous MUDs like AberMUD (which was in some very indirect way based on the original Bartle MUD code) and some similar projects (most notably Monster, a large extensible MUD written in Pascal for VMS), and I had a vague interest in building an interesting multi-user game, although at the time I'd figured what would be most interesting would be a multi-user game in the Rogue/Hack family. During the summer of 1989, the Internet Relay Chat system became popular among some of the CS grad students at CMU. On this system was a very simple multi-user Hunt the Wumpus game which routinely attracted dozens of players from all over the world. A friend of mine suggested that I hack up a small multi-user adventure game that would hang off of IRC and give these folks something more interesting to do. So in a weekend or so, drawing heavily on some of the features I knew about from the documentation of Monster, I put together the game and database part of TinyMUD. Another grad student supplied the telnet driver and we had a running prototype.

I'd figured that we'd just use the prototype to test the system out before putting in an IRC interface, but knowledge of its existence quickly leaked out to the Net and soon it was in heavy enough use that the IRC interface never seemed necessary.

About that same time Lars Penjl was working on what eventually became LPMud. I'm not sure quite what the state of LPMud (which was a much larger project) was when TinyMUD went up. I did talk to Lars briefly on TinyMUD and it sounded like LPMud was mostly ready to go at that point but that he hadn't fired it up because he hadn't worked out the kinks in his network driver. In any case, it was not more than two or three months before LPMud became available, which spawned most of the modern combat-oriented MUDs. LPMud also drew away most of the people who were interested in violence or achievement-oriented MUDs, leaving a more social crowd behind on the Tinys.

(Excerpted from an e-mail correpondence with the author.)

What Good Are They?

So this realm, like many others, splits into two factions. Though—oddly, for a crowd which loves to argue and *flame* (flames are heated arguments peppered with personal attacks) at the fine points of operating systems, computers and anything else that seems to arise—there is little interMUD bashing.

If these two philosophies show the main split, this is not to say that there aren't many variations on these themes. As Reid itemizes them.... "From 1990 onward the number of MUD programs in circulation increased rapidly. There are, among others, COOLMUDs, ColdMUDs, DikuMUDs, DUMs, LP-MUDs, MAGEs, MOOs, MUCKs, MUSEs, MUSHes, TeenyMUDs, TinyMUDs, UberMUDs, UnterMUDs, UriMUDs and YAMUDs (the latter being an acronym for 'yet another MUD')."

Net-Hype

And with the recent explosion of network awareness, the number of people using MUDs has expanded exponentially. The emergence of the Internet into the public awareness has brought the number of users to unprecedented levels.

Bruce Sterling, in his electronically distributed addendum/update to his book, *The Hacker Crackdown*, identifies the surge in networking consciousness:

> Similar public attention was riveted on the massive $22 billion megamerger between RBOC Bell Atlantic and cable-TV giant Tele-Communications, Inc. [since collapsed—wjs]. Nynex was buying into cable company Viacom International. BellSouth was buying stock in Prime Management, South-western Bell was acquiring a cable company in Washington DC, and so forth. By stark contrast, the Internet, a noncommercial entity which officially did not even exist, had no advertising budget at all. And yet, almost below the level of governmental and corporate awareness, the Internet was stealthily devouring everything in its path, growing at a rate that defied comprehension. Kids who might have been eager computer-intruders a mere five years earlier were now surfing the Internet, where their natural urges to explore led

them into cyberspace landscapes of such mindboggling vastness that the very idea of hacking passwords seemed rather a waste of time.

By 1993, there had not been a solid, knock 'em down, panic-striking, teenage-hacker computer-intrusion scandal in many long months. There had, of course, been some striking and well-publicized acts of illicit computer access, but they had been committed by adult white-collar industry insiders in clear pursuit of personal or commercial advantage. The kids, by contrast, all seemed to be on IRC, Internet Relay Chat.

With the linking of commercial systems on the Net, both small and large, came a more commercial—or, at least, non-academic-oriented—user, and the potential for these environments in business has presented itself.

There also seems to be an expectant feeling among users of these systems, as if they are onto something, and that somehow the future of networking will spawn from what is now happening in MUDS and IRC. Real-time interaction at little or low cost will find its uses.

But in the business world, with computers, it sometimes takes decades for a good idea to get general acceptance. Many companies only relatively recently got rid of their IBM punch cards. Many still may not have shaken the IBM punch card mindset.

The Next Phase

There are those who are trying to shape the future with MUDs. There's Jon Callas, whose system, Meeting Space, is attempting to provide MUD-type environments for business conferences.

In John December's electronic journal, *Computer-Mediated Communication Magazine* (September 1, 1994), network savant Chris Hand addressed the topic of serious MUDs for business in an article called "Meet me in Cyberspace:"

> MUDs used to be part of HackerSpace. They were populated by games-playing, programming Net-junkies who innocently spent their leisure time in a shared virtual space. Now things are changing. When a corporate colossus like Microsoft or Apple starts moving in, you know they must have smelled

money. Apple has announced eWorld, effectively a graphical front-end to a USENET-like BBS using a village, building and room metaphor for navigation. Microsoft's project Utopia is an experimental interface using a virtual house to organize activities. It doesn't take much to recognize these ventures for what they are—a tentative toe in the water of real-time interactive shared-space virtual communities: MUDs.

So when the big boys start moving into our cyberspace, what are we going to do? Run away and hide somewhere else? That's one option, but some of our Net pioneers have decided to meet them head-on.

Take Metaverse, for example. Run by Steve Jackson Games (well-known for taking on the establishment during Operation Sun Devil) under the umbrella of Illuminati Online, Metaverse is a subscription-based MOO. It also provides a home to several "virtual corporations," such as the Electronic Frontier Foundation, which have virtual office-space there.

This is one strategy: Net-citizens move their businesses into MUDspace now, before big business moves into MUDspace.

From a business point of view it makes sense. It costs money to physically transport people from A to B just so they can have a meeting. Driving on the roads is stressful and takes time (road traffic also kills thousands of people every year, as well as kicking out tons of pollution, but of course that's of no interest to your average capitalist venture). When you scale things up and start flying everywhere, the cost is even higher.

So Meeting Space lets you conduct virtual meetings across a network. Of course, this is useful, but it's nothing new—it's why we've had video-conferencing rammed down our throats as the Next Big Thing. The trouble with video is that it's expensive, it doesn't travel well over the Internet and who wants to sit in front of a camera for an hour trying to look awake anyway? The parallels with Orwell's telescreen are obvious.

MUDs as meeting-spaces have several advantages. If all you have to do is put a text window up on your screen, then you can carry on doing useful work during those long, boring meetings. There's no hassle with dragging someone in to record minutes when all you have to do is log the session into a file.

One of the great things about meeting in TextSpace is that no one can see you. This means that prejudices get left behind on the desktop: people have to judge you on your words rather than on your T-shirt, hair, gender or body odor. You are what you type. It also means that you can crawl out of bed, grab a cup of coffee and log in just in time for a meeting instead of rushing around like an idiot trying to get into the office—you don't even have to bother getting dressed.

This is an instant bonus for anyone running a small business on the Net, since it doesn't matter that you don't have offices bursting with palm trees and chrome. Get your ASCII right and you'll look just as good as anyone else doing the same thing. It goes without saying that anyone who finds it difficult to get from one place to another—whether they're physically disabled or just snowed in—can let their modem do the walking.

In "MUDs Grow Up: Social Virtual Reality in the Real World," Pavel Curtis— inventor of the MOO form of MUD—and David A. Nichols of Xerox's Palo Alto Research Center (the famous PARC Xerox facility, where microcomputing as it is known today was almost entirely visualized and prototyped, but whose parent company fumbled its marketing), describe their aims for the future of business uses of MUDs, though they think the medium must first move beyond text-only.

Unfortunately, text has significant drawbacks in a work environment. First, typing is much slower than speech for real-time communications. While most people can read faster than they can listen, they can speak much faster than they can type. In a world where telephones and face-to-face communications are readily available, real-time typing will not be a popular alternative.

Secondly, the aesthetic properties of text descriptions are largely wasted in a work setting. A worker's use of the computer is generally secondary to accomplishing some other task, and dramatic descriptions of the successful printing of a document, after victory over the evil forces of paper jams and toner spills, get old after awhile.

In addition to text-based interaction, therefore, we are adding real-time audio and video, and window-based graphical user interfaces. While typical MUDs assume that users have only a dumb terminal, we assume that they have digital audio and a graphics display, with optional video input. This is an increasingly realistic assumption, as almost all computers sold today (PCs, Macs, UNIX workstations) have graphics displays, and most either come with telephone-quality audio or can have it added cheaply (usually for about $100).

Curtis also reports on a project-in-progress called the "Astro-VR System," which is being designed for the NASA/JPL Infrared Processing and Analysis Center. Astro-VR would be a social virtual reality for the astronomers. "The system is intended to provide a place for working astronomers to talk with one another, give short presentations, and otherwise collaborate on astronomical research. In most cases, this system will provide the only available means for active collaboration at a level beyond electronic mail and telephones."

Other Uses

Business in MUDs doesn't necessarily mean *commerce*. There are those who see the potential of using the interactive atmospheres for enhancement of the individual. Two examples of such personal improvement MUDs currently being explored are for education and recovery missions.

Diversity University is one of a handful of budding educational entities recently detected online, striving to establish the first online distance schools. Diversity University (DU) exists nowhere else but online, and thus it exists nowhere else but in the minds of its founders and members.

Though education may be considered an ulterior motive for a university (a real one) to have a MUD online (since the students who program it, presumably, are educating themselves in programming techniques), there is a movement to make the MUD *be* the university. This kind of distance education, as its called, had been practiced for a few years, where some parts of a course are taken by interacting through electronic mail or the occasional real-time group MUD meeting. Soon it may be possible to follow entire certified courses of study without setting foot in a classroom, or a schoolhouse.

According to information distributed by DU:

> The ability to bring classes online is very appealing to many teachers. It allows them to demonstrate the power of the Global Information Infrastructure and show off its many forms, which include not only the acquisition of information, but also the interactive exchange of ideas with people from other cultural, political, and social environments.

Diversity University's Floor Plan.

```
              _____1_____          _____2_____         _____3_____
             _____                 _____JASON_ROAD____        _____(Jason's Ct.->)
            |  |                          .---------. |  Football field   | |  |                  | |  |
         6| |  |   Cllge of Agrcultr| |  |_____|  |  |   (Gym)      |  .----.  | |6
            |  |  |_____ ----- '|  ____BOB_STREET____         |  |              |  |Intrfaith| |  |
            |  |             Villa   |   Northern             |  |  |          |  | Center  | |  |
         5| |  |(grad dorm) Villekulla |  |   Quadrangle        |  |  (Pool) |  '----'| |5
            |  |_____|  |  |_____|  |  |          |_____|  |
            |  _____          ____7th_STREET____        _____
            |  |  |Cfetria|     _____|  |.----.f.----.|  |  .-._.-. .----.  |W|
         4|M|  |_____|  Dorm |Hum.|  ||Student|s| Admin|  |  |(          |  |  | |E|4
            |O|Hotel School  |  2  |Pot.|  ||Union |a|     |  |  |[ Library |  |Educatn| |S|
            |G|_____|---|____|  ||_____|/ '---'|  |[_____|  |  | |T|
            |U _____         ____LSU_STREET____   |.--.   '----'|H|
            |E|.-----..----.   |  |         |  ||Engl.|.--.::::::: E|
         3|'||  Business ||Communcatn\|H|         |S|  |   ||      |.--. |I|3
            |S|_____||____ ____|O|         |A|____||Cltrl||      | |M|
            | |.----. .----''--.|U| Southern Quad  |N|.--.|Studs|| Law  | |E|
            |R|Engin-|  | Tech Complex ||S|         |D|Hist.|__||____|| |R|
            |U|eering|  |  _____/|T|         |O|____||____|.--. | |
         2|N||_____| '-'.----.  |O|   flag|pole   |Z|.--. .--.|Poli | |S|2
            | |.-----.  | Medical ||N|         | ||    |_|Soc | Sci | |T|
            | ||Archtcture|  | Complex ||  |         |S|Psych_ Work| |____|/|R|
            | |'-----'  _____|  ||S|    .'N'.      |T|_-'_'--'_____| |I|
            | |(Construction .----. |  |T|    W-+-E      |    ____JEANNE'S_LANE____ P|
            | |.-. trailer) | Science | |  |    '.S.'      |  |.----.            | |
         1| ||__|<-'    |  Bldg. | |  |         |  || M&DA  | Ampithtr | |1
            |  |_____| '----' |  |         |  |'----'  |_____| |
            |_____6th_STREET_____|
                           1                          2                        3
```

But D U MOO's purpose is even greater than that. If you can imagine walking into a virtual chemistry lab and finding a virtual experiment waiting to be performed, then you are on the right track. We at DU think of it as an experiential learning project; educators refer to it as constructivism. You might be allowed to predict the results of an experiment to demonstrate the amount of base required to neutralize a specific amount of acid and then perform the experiment to determine the actual results. The program prompts you for an amount to add and then shows you a visual representation of what percentage of the neutralization has occurred. This process is continued until the base is completely neutralized.

If you prefer history to the sciences, you can take a virtual trip through time into a simulation of the 100 Year War. By logging onto the MOO using "connect peasant peasant" you will be brought onto the MOO at the beginning of the "war" and allowed to travel the path of one of the main combatants, witnessing the battles from the viewpoint of a local peasant.

MilMUDs

The military is looking into the issue of MUDs, according to Vic Moberg, of Naval Command, Control, and Ocean Surveillance Center Research. Moberg is sorting out how they could be used for virtual workgroups. "My particular interest is low bandwidth conferencing between ships at sea and shore sites. Other people at this facility are also looking into 'serious' MUDs, and are pursuing funding to establish one locally. I have heard, but cannot confirm, that Mitre is building a MUD for the USAF, presumably for conferencing. I personally am involved in satellite communications, with one of the goals being extension of Internet connectivity to select ships at sea. In this regard I am tasked to look into the communications requirements to provide various textual (e-mail, IRC, MUDs) and desktop video teleconferencing (VTC) services. My interest in setting up a conference area is as a testbed to look at the issue of required bandwidth (bits/second) versus utility. I would never expect an Admiral or ship's Captain to use a MUD for conferencing—they would have VTC available to them—but the more numerous lower-ranking positions, such as Supply Officers, Electronic Warfare Officers, and Communications Officers, might find it of benefit. MUDs are certainly less demanding on communications resources than even slow-scan TV, but if they aren't useful enough, there is no sense in offering them."

So from there the MUD phenomenon has come full circle. From the first internetworked SAGE shield, to Internet, then back to the military.

Recovery

A group hoping to help people cope with their *real life* problems is exploring another use for MUDs. Led by a Net traveler known as "Lady Squirrel," the group runs a MUD called Sanctuary.

"How much help goes on?" Lady Squirrel writes. "Well, I guess that would depend on your viewpoint, really. The people that come are people in abusive relationships, people who have survived rape and beatings, people who have survived and are still trying to come to terms with childhood abuse. Quite a few of the latter are MP (multiple personality).

These people all come here to meet up with 'like-minded' others. There are a couple of boards to post on, where they can write about their feelings, what they do when they are down. These boards help to try to bring themselves back up, write responses to others looking for help, and of course there's a general 'babble' board too. Every Tuesday evening (6 p.m. CST) we have a Gather...sort of a 'party,' and everyone brings virtual foods and drinks and games, and they just sit around and talk. I am working on trying to gain a federal grant for SANCTUARY...."

Resources

Where is all this computing power coming from? Previously, most MUDs existed on the machines of universities, either sanctioned, partially sanctioned, or underground. According to Aspnes, most MUDding in schools is regarded as a distraction to formal education.

The increase in commercial services accessing the network brought more computing resources online, but businesses run on tight margins and every CPU cycle must be made to count. So a sort of cyber real estate market has emerged, with folks who want to run a MUD—without access to abundant surplus educational resources—having to lease "space" on a commercial computer system. Even though life on the networks is expanding, resources seem to be tightening. Prices are all over the board at this point, with some reporting monthly fees of $20, while others report services asking as much as $450 per month. Though usership is expanding, the space available for new MUDs is at a premium.

Jacqueline Hamilton is the head administrator of Harper's Tale MOO: "There are practically no pay sites available. I've had maybe three possibilities for pay sites. As it is, yes, we're having an extremely hard time finding a better site. The MOO has certain requirements. At present ours takes 20-25 megs of RAM, plus maybe 20 megs of disk space. It also must run on a UNIX machine connected directly to the Internet."

Besides difficulty finding sites, there can be problems once a site is found. Site instability can cause your favorite MUD to jump about the Net. Changing addresses often can be frustrating for both administrator and user. "We've moved three times," says Hamilton. "First, we outgrew our initial site. The second time, the lag (delays caused by heavy network computer traffic) and my mistrust of the site admin led me to move to a more secure .edu site. Our MOO has been there for a long time, but had to recently and unexpectedly leave due to political problems at the university in question. Now we're running on a site in Croatia. It's the only thing that was offered. We're still trying to move back to the States; the transatlantic lag is often extremely bad."

Just as with everything else, there are politics involved in MUDs too, though for Hamilton, real-world Balkan instability had nothing to do with it. One site had to be given up because of "the internal politicking at the university itself, and the potential risk to our benefactor sys admin's [system administrator's] job. The choice was pretty clear: get rid of the MOO to save his job. It's one reason I don't like .edu sites. They're never permanent."

As for resources, though, many MUD administrators take what they can get. James R. Owens runs a MUSH based at the University of Buffalo: "My resource/machine is basically a scrap machine. When the university's new fileserver came in, they moved the old one to a back room and let people use it for testing/projects. I got to be one of those lucky people."

On the other hand, David Paris, who runs Valhalla on a commercial site, says the problem is not lack of sites. "Finding a site for a MUD is pretty easy. There are loads of machines out there on the Net with all kinds of folks who have access to them. Unfortunately, finding a stable site for a MUD is damned difficult. Let's face it, MUDs consume vast quantities of expensive resources. No business or university that is actually aware of a MUD's existence and usage tends to want it around (there are some exceptions, but from a simply practical standpoint, MUDs aren't school, and they don't make money)." Paris reports that his MUD has had seven sites over the last four years, plus "lots of other site-related 'incidents.'"

"If you want a stable site, you have to build it yourself. It's not cheap. It's not easy."

Where the Fun Is

Though MUD space for business and education is on the rise, for most, there need be no other reason for a MUD than, well, fun. Bartle says he's been plagued by "these 'we have to find some non-entertaining use for MUDs to justify their existence' people, an attitude which has dogged me since the project began, and the reason I gave up my post at University to work on MUDs privately. Entertainment is a valid use for MUDs!"

This is not to say that even the gaming MUDs are all hack-and-slash, swords and sorcery. Some "games" simulate certain aspects of real life. HoloMUCK, for example, gives new meaning to the phrase "low-level character." New players there start at, well… here's the opening screen…

```
                              Welcome to
  ___   ___        .___           ____   ___     ____           ___.
 /   |  \__|____   |  |   ____    /     \ |    \ _/ ___\|  |/ _|
/    ~  (  <_> ) |_(  <_> )   Y     \   |   /\   \___|  |  <
\    Y  /  \___/|___/\__  \___|  /____/ \___  /____|_  \
 \___|_ /  \___/|___/\__  \___|  /____/ \___  /____|_  \
       \/              \/              \/         \/       \/

    —=<     WHO == show all the users who are currently online    >=—
    —=<    QUIT == disconnects from the server without logging on  >=—
    —=< connect <name> <pass> = connect to an existing character >=—
    —=<   connect guest guest = connect to the guest character    >=—
    —=<   Mail sjade@collatz.mcrcim.mcgill.edu for a character     >=—

connect guest guest
————————————[ Game_Manager's MOTD ]————————————
Please alert a wizard immediately if ANY room you dig is parented to #0.

[Guest1]  You feel as though an old friend has returned.


The Homeless Shelter(#22Rna)
You wake up in the town's Homeless Shelter, where vagrants are put for protective holding.
Please don't sleep in public places—there are plenty of open apartments available. Type
'apartments' to see how to get to an apartment building with open vacancies.
There is a small sign on the wall here, with helpful information.  Type 'look sign' to
read it.
The door is standing open for your return to respectable society.  Simply walk 'out' to
the center.
Your pager beeps.  Type 'page' to receive the message.
```

Other Worlds

There are also science fiction worlds, both from the Cyberpunk genre inspired by William Gibson, and the more low-tech universe conjured up by Anne McCaffrey's Dragonriders of Pern Series, Harper's Tale is a Pern MUD. "There are several Perns, mostly MUSHes, two MOOs," says Hamilton. "Anne McCaffrey is a well-known sci-fi/fantasy writer. Pern is a colony world settled by humans; it's low-tech and agrarian, but the main attraction is the dragons. People can impress a dragon when it hatches, thereby becoming emotionally and telepathically linked to the dragon for the rest of their lives. Pern depends on dragonriders to protect it from 'thread,' an alien organism that falls from the skies and eats anything organic in its path. Only fire (the dragons breathe fire) and water will kill thread. Dragons, and perhaps the low-tech aspect, probably appeal most to people who play Pern games."

Fur

And most unusual of all is an activity that occurs nowhere, except maybe in the works of Loony Tunes and certain other children's television shows. There is a large mass of people who come online to act like cute cartoon animals. The general label for the "hobby" is "Fur" and the practitioners frequent a MUD called FurryMUCK, and many like-minded other MUD sites.

According to Simon Raboczi, the world of Fur is "an example of a subculture which is nigh-invisible in RL [real-life], but somehow comes into its own via WAN [the network]. The nebulous focus is around art and literature involving talking animals."

Endless Possibilities

In a Usenet conference area, new MUDgoer William Mize, a struggling novelist, posted a list of topics he'd like to see covered by MUD:

MUDs I'd Like to See:

1. **LOVECRAFTMUD**—Based on the works of H P Lovecraft. Explore creepy old houses and ancient ruins. Meet weird people, encounter dangerous beasts, and lose sanity points.

2. **MYSTERYMUD**—Lightning cracks outside the door and the rain comes down as you and the other guests settle in for the night. Someone has been killed and the phone lines are down until morning. Will daylight come before the murderer strikes again, or can you and your group find out who it is and save the day?

3. **UNIVERSAL/HAMMER MUD**—Based on the black and white horror movies of the 30s through the 60s: Dracula, The Creature, The Mummy, etc. The man you just met said his name was Dr. Anton Phibes, but you thought he was dead. What do you do?

4. **SPRINGFIELD MUD**—It's the town to be in. Go down to Moe's and have a drink or place a bet or listen to Aerosmith, have Mrs. Krabaple slip you her phone number, watch Homer chase Bart around, make a pass at Marge or Principal Skinner.

5. **GOTHAMMUD**—<cue Danny Elfman music> It's the home of Batman and just about any other superhero you can think of. Yeah, it's artistic license, but New York is SOOOO boring, huh? :> Be a Hero. Be a Villain. Join the Avengers or The Legion of Super Heroes.

As a fiction writer, Mize feels an affinity toward the MUDs, where creation is on the fly and interactive: "Regarding MUDs, I would think that the only limitations would be the person's imagination. Fantasy worlds have tended to be the focus of the MUDs, I think, for two reasons. One—a lot of programmers are science fiction and fantasy fans. They are passionate about this genre and one should always deal with one's passions in as many facets as possible. Two—which is easier to escape into? A land of hobbits and wizards and elves, or a land of corporate executives and secretaries and stock markets? Which gives the bigger payoff? Payoff in terms of relaxation, adventure, escapism, etc.?

"Me, personally, I like my dollops of fantasy and science fiction with a good helping of nostalgia. Hence my love for the old pulps, old Universal monster movies and the like. Sometimes you must look to the past for inspiration into the future."

There have also been indications that some MUD topics in development include: Ancient Egypt, The American Frontier (Wild West) and World War II as interpreted through the pages of the comic books. Personally, this observer considers the "killer" topic for a MUD, either to make a bundle of money or just to get lots of attention, would have to be the worlds of F.L. Baum, more commonly known as the site of an Emerald City, which houses the Wizard of Oz.

With tight resources or resistant administrators, one gets the feeling that the history of networking has been leading up to this, and that the almost palpable feeling of expectancy online exists because everyone knows that this is just an intermediate phase.

The best of MUD is yet to come.

Chapter 3

Online Fundamentals

the dawn of the computer networking age (which we are now experiencing) requires ever-dwindling amounts of technical knowledge for the reasonably intelligent, interested party. The techniques needed to master the nets offer no more stretch for the mind than what might be needed to maintain an automobile and the addresses of your best friends and favorite hangouts (and that's as close to the motor-transport cliché metaphor as I'll come in this volume).

Think of the current situation as, perhaps, the late Iron Age of the Information Era—the tools you are about to encounter seem primitive compared to all the recent hype. Up until recently, these networks were not intended for general public consumption (and even now they seem to have backed into that reluctantly). Scientists and researchers do not mind working with naked text. It's efficient. The wider the net is cast, the more pretty pictures are needed to hold the public's interest. Graphics-based MUDs are hatching. There's one called *DragonSpires*, which may bloom into a full-tilt online service sometime in the future. At this writing, it's an experiment looking for backers. They're starting to swarm.

Getting where you're going will be a simple matter, requiring only diligent application of common sense, and awareness of the basic rules of connection. In this section we'll cover the basics of Internet communications:

- Telnet—for real-time connections.
- FTP for file transferring.
- Usenet, a most useful set of messaging forums where the latest information can be found.
- The World Wide Web, a burgeoning format for network searching, of which some MUD folks are taking full advantage.
- And a bit about client/server, the theoretical computing model on which most of this action is based.

Telnet

Unless your system is equipped with a MUD *client*—specially adapted "front-end" software that can connect all its users with a particular type of MUD—most of your everyday MUD interaction will occur using **telnet**.

Telnet is the TCP/IP protocol's terminal emulator, meaning it allows a user from anywhere on the network to use a computer anywhere else on the same network. If the user has an account, that remote host can be accessed as though it were sitting in the same room. The only noticeable variable is an occasional time lag caused by network traffic in between. You'll hear a lot about lag on the network. Certain peak periods (Friday nights, for instance) are worse than others.

Telnet, though, has some drawbacks. As a generic terminal emulator, it doesn't provide word wrap, something users of any decent word-processing system have come to expect. Word wrap is the calculation that allows a word processor to decide when to move a word at the end of a line down to the next line, keeping it whole. Many clients for MUD use provide this feature. Telnet also lacks a text buffer, so if someone sends a message that is displayed on your screen while you're typing, it will break up your text. Once you press **enter**, though, the line you were composing will be sent intact, and printed out on your screen whole.

With telnet, a user can transport his or her presence to far-flung systems all over the world. It's as simple as issuing the command **telnet**, then the **<siteaddress>** at that prompt on most host systems. Other systems require the format **open <siteaddress>** at the **telnet** prompt. Look on your own host system for information about how it's done. Or if you find yourself at a command prompt, type in **telnet** and see what happens.

Site addresses usually adhere to the basic format. For instance, with a MUD site, it might be:

```
mudname.hostcomputer.domain XXXX
```

where **XXXX** is (usually) a four-digit port number. Notice the space between the address and the port number.

The address gives all information to the system about where to route the information packets that maintain your connection. Ports are individual access slices of the remote system's internal "socket" matrix. It's a further refinement for an address to a computer that may be in use for many other purposes besides the MUD you're visiting.

Guest Logon

Most sites allow *guest* logons. At the prompt, you would type **"guest"** and when asked for a password, you may type **"visitor."** Sometimes the combination is **"logon name guest"** and **"password guest"**. Often the word **"new"** can be used to gain guest access. The opening screen of nearly all MUDs, though, will provide information on what to do. If you see no such information, or if **logon** doesn't seem to be working (even though you see a **logon** prompt), then more often than not you forgot to add the port number at the end of the address. Check for this and try again.

Telnet Sample

A visit to a sample site partway across the world should suffice. Say you live in Washington, D.C., and you want to know how to use that city's Metro subway system to pop over to Alexandria, Virginia. You don't have your Metro map handy. But your computer is networked.

There's an Internet site that can help you. It's located in Paris, France, as part of the network system shared by two universities—Université Piérre et Marie Curie and Université Denis Diderot.

Get online and find your telnet facility. You may end up with a prompt like this:

```
telnet>
```

Type in the address:

```
metro.jussieu.fr 10000
```

Here's what you'll see:

```
Bienvenue sur le serveur d'itineraires  : Welcome to the subway navigator
des metros.                             :
Grace a ce service, vous pouvez         : This service may help you find a
chercher un parcours en metro dans      : route in the subway of some cities
certaines villes du monde.              : in the world.

Adressez vos commentaires a :           : Comments to:
    Pierre.David@prism.uvsq.fr          :     Pierre.David@prism.uvsq.fr

Parametres du terminal :                : Terminal settings:
    Interruption : ^C                   :     Interrupt  : ^C
    Correction   : [Backspace] ou [DEL] :     Correction : [Backspace] or [DEL

Vous pouvez demander de l'aide pour     : You can ask for help in all
chaque question en tapant '?'.          : questions with '?'.
Les reponses par defaut sont indiquees  : Default answers are listed within
encadrees par des crochets '[...]'      : square brackets '[...]'
N'utilisez pas de caracteres accentues  : Don't use accented characters.

Version 1.4, (c) Pierre David/Janick Taillandier, 1990-93

Quelle langue desirez-vous ?            : Which language do you want to use ?
Votre choix ? (Francais/Anglais)        : Your choice ? (French/English)
Choix/Choice [English] :
```

This site gives screens in two languages. Choose a city:

```
Choose a city among these ones:
austria/vienna          india/calcutta
canada/montreal         italy/milano
canada/toronto          italy/palermo
czech/prague            mexico/mexico
france/lille            netherlands/amsterdam
france/lyon             spain/barcelona
france/marseille        spain/madrid
france/paris            sweden/stockholm
france/toulouse         united-kingdom/london
germany/berlin          usa/atlanta
germany/bonn-koln       usa/boston
germany/frankfurt       usa/chicago
germany/munich          usa/new-york
greece/athens           usa/san-francisco
hong-kong/hong-kong     usa/washington

Your choice [france/paris] : usa/washington

The network includes all Washington D.C. Metrorail subway stations.

Source : From a december 1993 map supplied by R. Holland and Richard Hudson.
```

Type in your departure station:

```
DUPONT CIRCLE
```

Then type in your arrival station:

```
KING STREET
```

Here's what you'll see:

```
Estimated time = 30 minutes

Line Red, Direction 'Wheaton'
        Dupont Circle
        Farragut North
        Metro Center
        Gallery Place/Chinatown
Line Yellow, Direction 'Huntington'
        Gallery Place/Chinatown
        Archives/Navy Memorial
        L'Enfant Plaza
        Pentagon
        Pentagon City
        Crystal City
        National Airport
        Braddock Road
        King Street

Do you want to continue [Yes] : n

Do you want to send a message to the author [No] :
```

It tells you to get on the Red Line train heading for Wheaton, get off at the Gallery Place/China Town station and board a Yellow Line train bound for Huntington. All the stations along the way are listed. The trip should take 30 minutes.

It's not hugely interactive, but as a simple example, it will do.

Making the telnet connection will prove to be the simplest of transactions after the first few tries. Try it with a MUD called Island. The telnet address is **teaching4.physics.ox.ac.uk 2092**.

As you may surmise from the address, you would be logging on to a MUD running on a computer owned by the Physics Department of Oxford University, United Kingdom.

FTP

FTP stands for *File Transfer Protocol*, and with it you can dig into online repositories (FTP sites) full of information and software for nearly every desire. Once into the directory structures of these sites, you can **download** (using the strangely intuitive command **get**) to take the file back to your host system. From there, getting it home to your own computer will differ according to the details of your local host. In a system like Netcom and most institutional systems, you'll have a directory of your own onto which you can build your own subdirectory structure. That's also where these FTPed files will most likely be placed when they are **gotten** during the FTP transfer. On Delphi Internet, the file will be sent to your *workspace*, a storage area all members have for their personal files and mail. From there, use the regular downloading techniques you'd use for retrieving any file. Check the documentation at your site for the exact procedures.

This process is referred to as *anonymous FTP*. It is not entirely anonymous, since most systems will take your user name and system into their logs.

You can also use FTP to **post** (or upload) files to a site. For this you would use the (oddly intuitive) command call **put**. If you should ever have occasion to be holding something you think others would be interested in, be it a program or text file, check with the policies of the target system to see how to **put** and what sort of information is acceptable at that site. Many sites have restrictions of one sort or another.

Why would you need FTP? With an FTP session, you can get informative *FAQ* files. A FAQ is a document constructed mostly by contributors of a Usenet newsgroup, sometimes by others. These documents serve as a reference source for the group, so that the most common questions asked by newcomers need not be rehashed more than once.

You will also need FTP to acquire software that will make your online life a little more enjoyable, such as the client program for *DragonSpires*, kept at ftp.eden.com, as you'll see in the sample below.

How Does It Go?

The general order of FTP action is common to all systems:

1. Dial-up or access your **local network host**.

2. Get to the **FTP** prompt on that system.

3. Type in the **remote FTP site network address**.

4. **Navigate** around the directories on the remote host.

5. **Locate files** you want.

6. **Transfer** (**get**) the files to your personal storage area on your local host system.

7. Leave the FTP site by typing **bye**.

8. Take the files from the storage area and either download them (if you are in a dial-up) or otherwise **move them** to where you will be working on them locally.

Sample FTP

Find the FTP facility on your system. You may end up at a prompt that looks like this:

```
FTP>
```

Then type the *FTP site address*. Again, as with telnet, many systems will require the command **open** be used before the address:

```
open ftp.eden.com
```

The remote system may greet you with a request:

```
Enter username (default: anonymous):
```

If you don't have an account on the target FTP system and if your host system doesn't provide a default as above, type in:

```
anonymous
```

The system will ask for a *password*:

```
Enter password [BILL_S@DELPHI.COM]:
```

If you do not have an account on the system and your host system doesn't provide a default, type in your e-mail address as the password, for logging purposes. Next should be the site's opening screen. This may sometimes hold information about the site and how it is managed:

```
220 matrix.eden.com FTP server (Version wu-2.4(4)) Fri Jul 22
23:46:09 CDT
ready.
331 Guest login ok, send your complete e-mail address as pass-
word.
230-
*****************************************************************************
230-                    Welcome to the Eden Matrix FTP server.
230-
230-     If you have any comments or problems, please email
jher@eden.com.
230-                    There are 1 users out of max 5.
230-
*****************************************************************************
230-
230-Please read the file README
230-  it was last modified on Fri Sep 30 18:52:04 1994-36 days
ago
230 Guest login ok, access restrictions apply.
```

The numbers on the left are operating system identifiers and won't concern us at all.

```
FTP> pwd
```

pwd is the **present working directory** command. You can get your bearings by using it. In this instance, since we just logged on, it results in:

```
257 "/" is current directory.
The remote working directory is /
```

This slash refers to the base or *root* directory. Use this command anywhere to see in which directory you are currently.

To move up in the directory tree (or down deeper into the system, to the next level of directories), use the **cd** command, for **change directory**.

```
FTP> cd pub
```

Most public files are kept somewhere under the *pub* subdirectory. In this instance we know that the *DragonSpires* client software is in the **/pub/dspire** directory.

To see what's in the pub directory, use the **ls -l** command (which stands for "list contents in long format").

```
FTP> ls -l
```

This will result in an on screen accounting of the directory contents:

```
200 PORT command successful.
150 Opening ASCII mode data connection for /bin/ls.
total 12
drwxr-xr-x  3 0     666   512 Oct 18 17:04 cuseeme
drwxr-xr-x  2 1175  2323  512 Oct 29 23:24 dspire
drwxr-xr-x  2 0     2323  512 Oct 26 17:12 eden
drwxrwxr-x  6 0     2323  512 Oct  2 04:19 mac
drwxr-xr-x  4 0     2323  512 Sep 21 06:19 pc
drwxr-xr-x  2 0     2323  512 Oct 27 08:26 unix
226 Transfer complete.
```

These are all directories that split off into categories for classifying files. The *d* at the left signifies that the line represents a *directory*. The *rwx* strings on the left tell about permission for the directory: who can read, write, and execute them. This system applies to files, as well, but is of no immediate concern to "anonymous" visitors like us, since all files in public directories are available for public plundering, so to speak, and the permissions will be set accordingly. For more detail on permissions, check with your nearest UNIX geek or reference book. Also shown above are some storage numbers and the dates and times the files were last altered by their owners.

If the -l had been left off the command, the readout of the directories would have looked like this:

```
FTP> ls
200 PORT command successful.
150 Opening ASCII mode data connection for file list.
mac
unix
dspire
pc
cuseeme
eden
```

which would have served just as well, except that in directories containing files *and* other directories, it may be difficult to tell the difference between them at times.

These directories split off seekers of Mac, PC-compatible, and UNIX items. The top line of the listing is for *CUSeeMe*, a system for sending live feed video across the Net. One directory is for the Eden host system and the other is the one we came for, **/dspire**. Change to it:

```
FTP> cd dspire
```

And let's see what's in it:

```
FTP> ls -l
200 PORT command successful.
150 Opening ASCII mode data connection for /bin/ls.total 1076
-rw-r-r-  1 1175   2323   277210 Oct 25 12:45 dspir14c.zip
-rw-r-r-  1 1175   2323    99855 Oct 29 18:31 hlloween.zip
-rw-r-r-  1 1175   2323    48162 Oct 27 16:34 knig0003.gif
-rw-r-r-  1 1175   2323    38311 Oct  9 22:31 marbled2.gif
-rw-r-r-  1 1175   2323    61113 Oct 25 12:51 up14-14c.zip
```

At this writing, the most recent version of the *DragonSpires* client is 1.4c. That's the top file listed. Also in the directories are some *gifs (graphics files)* and a compressed *zip file* (see below) having to do with a Halloween variant of the game. The bottom file is a program that will upgrade an earlier version of the client to version 1.4c.

Since this is a compressed zip file, some parts of it are *binary*. In other words, there is computer code contained in them that is not represented by a text equivalent. And so the file must be retrieved in FTP *binary* mode.

To change the mode, type **binary** at the prompt, and the system will acknowledge that you've changed the method to be used for transfer:

```
FTP> binary
200 Type set to I.
```

Use the **get** command to grab that client file:

```
FTP> get dspire14c.zip
200 PORT command successful.
150 Opening BINARY mode data connection for dspir14c.zip (277210
bytes).
226 Transfer complete.
250 CWD command successful.
```

Now beat it out of there:

```
FTP> bye
221 Goodbye.
|FTP| Returning to host system....
```

That's all there is to it.

Long File Names

Some file names you'll see in the FTP mix may be bigger and stranger than you may be used to in MS-DOS and some other microcomputer platforms. UNIX and TCP/IP allow for longer file names and multiple divisions within them. If you want to take a file back to your MS-DOS-based system, at some point it will have to be renamed according to the proper "8-dot-3" file name rule. Sometimes, as on Delphi Internet, the intervening host will rename the file for you.

Character Case

In FTP, be sure to use uppercase letters when the file name contains them. The file may not come to you otherwise. In addition, any file or directory name that has any uppercase text or special characters, such as hyphens, will probably require that the file or directory name be enclosed in quote marks. For instance, that *dspir14c.zip* file used in the previous example had no such characters, so it didn't need quotes. If it had been listed as *Dspr-14c.zip* for some reason, however, the command to get it would have had to be:

```
FTP> get "Dspi-14c.zip"
```

This also applies to changing into directories (cd) that have the same kind of characters.

File Compression and Archiving

Compressed archives come in many flavors. Various and incompatible file shrinking and bundling methods are available. The *DragonSpires* program is in *PKZIP* format, a popular technique for packing and shrinking in the PC-compatible world. Other methods are more common to UNIX systems.

The various brands of compression used on a group of files are identified by some segment of the file name, most often the last segment.

If a file is named *files.tar.Z*, for instance, it means that the individual files were stuck together with the UNIX program *tar*, and then compressed with the UNIX Z compression algorithm. Using the same programs on the resulting file will open it and uncompress the files inside. Some other compression methods more familiar to the PC world are *ARJ* and *LZH*.

The files in the archive are useless until they are returned to their original state using the compatible process for unarchiving and uncompressing them.

Below is a list of "labels" you might see in or near the end of a file name. Each identifies a type of archive and/or compression method. The programs you use to decompress files in these formats will usually be found in a directory named *compression* on any FTP site containing software for your computing platform:

extender	program
.arc	archived with PKPAK.EXE
.arj	archived with ARJ.EXE
.lbr	libraried with LU.EXE
.lzh	archived with LHA.EXE
.zip	archived with ZIP.EXE
.zoo	archived with ZOO.EXE
.?q?	squeezed files (middle letter is a Q. '?' is a wild card representing any character.)
.gz	compressed with gzip
.Z	compressed with compress

Command Summary for basic FTP. Keep this handy during FTP sessions:

Command	Action
cd <directory name>	Change directory (downward).
cdup (or cd ..)	Change directory (upward).
ls -l (or dir)	List directory contents.
get <filename> <newname>	Transfer a file to you; change the name in the process.
put <from filename> <to filename>	Transfer a file from you to the FTP site.
mget <filename> <filename>, etc.	Transfer multiple files to you.
CONTROL-S	Stop scrolling.
CONTROL-Q	Restart scrolling.

MUD Clients

Client/server is a general term for the division of computing duties among locations on a network. Generally speaking, a large, well-outfitted central computer that handles files for a network may be declared a *file server*. Often, calculations required for graphics presentation locally will be handled by the local computer, the *client*, in the data exchange relationship. The practice of client/server is embodied in the Internet, with every computer acting more or less as both server and client for every other computer. An individual user machine, whether it's a console attached directly to a host system or dialing up through a modem, is generally classified as a client.

Various features of the network landscape, such as MUDs and IRC, can be thought of as adhering to a client/server structure, as well. A host computer handles nearly all the housekeeping duties, and the user's local computer accesses the central machine at will, performing only those chores necessary to maintain contact and to provide a terminal for the outlying users.

One of the items you might use FTP to get is a MUD client program. A client is custom-made for accessing a particular type of MUD and is built to provide some amenities not available with telnet. Some clients also provide *macros*, which allow several commands and preset remarks or actions to be put into a few keystrokes. Some also have features for filtering out messages from unwanted fellow players (there's a certain amount of incivility here, as in Usenet. Shutting your ears electronically to the messages of the pests around you is known as *gagging*.) Some clients help a player build new areas on the MUD.

Most clients must be installed (*compiled* is the term normally used) in the host system, not on an individual computer. It would be wise to get the permission and assistance of your system administrator before installing one. The majority run on UNIX. Some run on Macintosh. Some run under VMS and other systems.

The MUD FAQ maintained by Jennifer Smith, in addition to lots of other useful information about MUDs, can be referred to for a detailed, up-to-date listing of MUD client and server software. It can be found at the site **ftp.math.okstate.edu** in the **pub/muds/misc** directory as **mud-faq**. The client/server portion of the FAQ is included in the Appendix of this book.

FTP sites that hold clients and other software useful to mudders include:

ftp.math.okstate.edu	ftp.white.toronto.edu
parcftp.xerox.com	ftp.lysator.liu.se
ftp.tcp.com	ftp.princeton.edu

Usenet

Usenet is the cluster of messaging conference "areas," or *newsgroups*, that you'll encounter on most Internet-connected systems. There are thousands of groups, each discussing a different topic or variation of a topic. It's not exactly real-time interactive, but some of the newsgroup topics are related to the interactive activities on the Net. The groups can be a good source of up-to-date information. Some are the first place a MUD administrator will go to announce a new system, or to announce a change in an old favorite.

Usenet newsgroups follow an hierarchy system of classification, which flows from the general to the specific. Some newsgroups have the word *rec* in their names. These are the groups on *recreational topics*. A newsgroup is made up of *articles*, which are the messages posted by users. Some can contain FAQs, which are posted on a regular basis.

Some basics to remember:

1. Watch for a FAQ giving the basic information that everyone who subscribes to the newsgroup is assumed to understand, sometimes strictly so. Many Usenet groups, for some reason, have attracted a bevy of crabby users who *flame* anyone at any opportunity. (*Flame* is a new word for what, in other media, might be called a "nasty letter" or a "crank phone call." On USENET it's almost institutionalized.) The most frequent targets of flames are newcomers who posts messages that make them appear too much like, well...like newcomers. Most advice on Net participation will tell you to *lurk* in the group before posting an article. This may be a good idea at times, but the feeling here is that if the channels are meant to be made available to all, then that would include newcomers, too. Join in if you feel like it, but be prepared for some unfriendly types to attack you for no apparent reason, other than that they've never seen your name before.

2. Use news readers or off-line mail readers. Some systems have news reader client facilities online to make reading newsgroups easier. These allow systematic, if not easy, tracking, scanning, and searching of groups for topic streams known as *threads*. These readers also

facilitate responding. Some regular, dial-up bulletin board systems (BBSs) also carry newsgroups along with their ordinary local discussions and networked messaging *echoes*. Many of these systems link users with their mail though a system of *mail doors* and readers. A *door* is software on the BBS that organizes the mail and sends it to the user during a session. The reader, which is on the user's system, has the same kind of organizing, searching, and responding features as the Internet-style news readers.

MUD/IRC Newsgroups

At this writing, the MUD/IRC-related newsgroups carried on the Net include these:

MUDS

alt.flame.mud

alt.mud

alt.mud.bsx

alt.mud.chupchups

alt.mud,german

alt.mud.lp

alt.mud.cyberworld

alt.mud.moo

alt.mudders.anonymous

rec.games.mud.admin

rec.games.mud.announce

rec.games.mud.diku

rec.games.mud.lp

rec.games.mud.misc

rec.games.mud.tiny

rec.games.mud.bogleg.eotl.bume

de.alt.mud

IRC

alt.irc

alt.irc.announce

alt.irc.hottub

alt.irc.ircii

alt.irc.questions

alt.irc.undernet

alt.irc.opers

alt.irc.recovery

alt.irc.bot

chile.irc

no.irc

usm.inf.irc

WWW

The hottest activity on the Net these days involves a search method known a *World Wide Web*, or WWW, or 3W. Based on a system of linkages called the *Hypertext Mark-Up Language* (HTML), WWW has developed into the most "surfable" mode of network usage so far. It's another case of client/server, in which the network hosts perform the mundane tasks of searching and sorting, and your own computer—or the system at the service you call—displays and formats the resulting text and graphic information.

Using the World Wide Web is like *browsing* through all the information in the world, and that's why client software packages used to accomplish it are called *browsers*. The most prominent of these is *NCSA Mosaic*. Another is the text-based *Lynx*, and that is what you'll see on Pipeline:

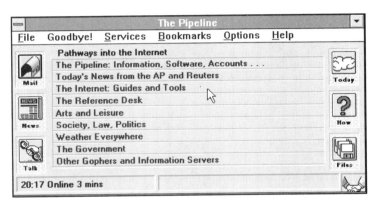

To get to the Web on Pipeline, choose "Internet Guides and Tools." Then, from the menu of features, choose "Lynx":

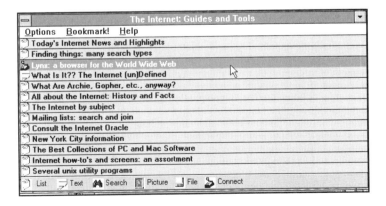

The Lynx browser will show its opening page:

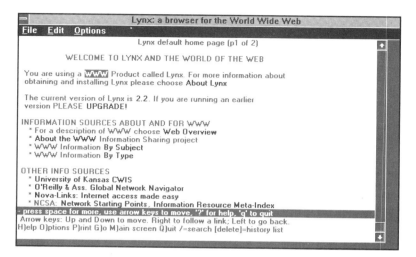

What does any of this have to do with MUDs? Well, at the input line on the bottom of the page, there's a place for typing in an *URL* (Uniform Resource Locator). That's another type of network address. Use an URL to tell the WWW on which *homepag*e you would like to start your journey. This URL,

```
http://www.cis.upenn.edu/~lwl/mudinfo.html
```

points to an extensive MUD-oriented WWW page maintained by Lydia Leong at the University of Pennsylvania.

And this one:

```
http://math.okstate.edu/~jds/mudfaqs.html
```

is a WWW version of Jennifer Smith's MUD FAQ.

Type in a **G,** for **go**, at the prompt and then input the URL as is... ...and a hypertext smorgasbord of MUD information awaits.

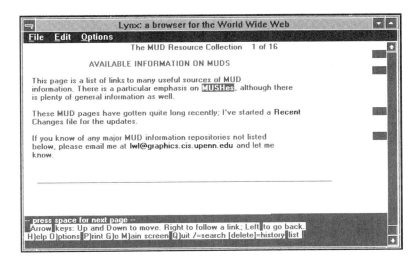

The gray rectangle around the word MUSHES, above, indicates that that is the current, active link. Choosing it will send you off to a place with more information on MUSHES. Each path and destination may have other, subsequent links to follow. Ad infinitum. So, off you go.

Now, with these tools, you are equipped to find information about MUDs, find your way into MUDs, and retrieve information and useful software tools for MUDding. Seasoned netheads will have skipped most of it. Newcomers can use these tools not only for MUD interaction, but for accessing the Internet in many other contexts and for many other purposes.

Chapter 4

Behavior

though such multi-user environments as MUDs are by no means new, more than ten years' development in a new medium is not enough time to predict its final form. As in any medium in flux, no broad standards of behavior can be applied in every case. In fact, some regard the opportunities afforded by MUDs as a way of conducting life *without* standards at all. There are MUDs in which the wizards couldn't care less how their users go about their activities; and the morass of IRC, with its uncontrolled, border-crossing open rivers, rivulets and, yes, sewers of running conversation may represent the most widely participated, bloodshedless anarchy yet known to civilization.

Even so, trends are taking shape, and the wider awareness of online life has brought increased interest by both law enforcement and various other "real-life" institutions.

Behavior online at this point, as far as MUDs are concerned, breaks down into three main areas: *In Character* behavior (IC), *Out of Character* behavior (OC), and MUD attacks.

System administrators and MUD wizards in charge of the server facilities deal with internal problems in various ways. *In Character* justice—which deals with the players "playing" in the game and how they behave—may be a bit less serious but no less graphically lethal in some instances, though a player killed off in the context of the game is always welcome to return with a new character. This is not necessarily so in *Out of*

Character situations, which may involve issues of harassment of other players and disruption of the equilibrium of the MUD itself.

Out of Character Behavior

OC, or Out of Character, issues fall under the basic laws governing system administrators everywhere, not just on MUDs. But only on MUDs is it normal for these folks to openly call themselves *gods*. Their beat includes the possibility of misuse of the systems, harassment of other users, and other attempts to disrupt otherwise peaceful online environments. Every system and MUD is different in what is tolerable for the users. There is no guarantee that the MUD gods or IRC *ops* (operators) will care much about any single user's problems with another user.

Sometimes life online can take a rough turn.

By and large, though, you can count on some form of action from a MUD god or wizard for:

- Relentless harassment of another user.

- Operating multiple characters simultaneously.

- Abuse of the "chat" or "shout" command to the detriment of online peace.

- Attempts to hack or disrupt the MUD by exploiting known bugs.

Harassment is a judgment call, and many wizards are inclined to let the chips fall where they may. Users are not required to visit MUDs in which they feel the admins are not responsive to their complaints, however, and the number of MUDs has grown so quickly recently that there's a wide choice of standards. Those who like a more civil atmosphere will avoid the rowdiness of hack and slash MUDs and those who must play at killing for fulfillment will find their online homes.

MUD gods and wizards are ready to defend their causes.

Harassment comes in many forms, from the *hard tail*—when a user follows another around for no apparent reason, making rude and possibly obscene comments—to the possibly unwelcome attention that a user with an apparently female-sounding name (or female-*presenting*, whether actually female or not) can attract.

The overwhelming majority of males on the Net makes for a dicey situation for the unsuspecting female. A female-sounding name will attract special attention, some welcome and some not. Wizards may favor female characters, wanting to keep them around.

There are also men who deliberately name their characters to sound like females, ostensibly for experimentation in gender roles. This leads to another form of harassment, which may occur to an authentic female with a female-sounding user name.

Pavel Curtis addresses this topic in "Mudding: Social Phenomena in Text-Based Virtual Realities" (a paper available electronically under the file name, **diac92.txt** at many MUD-related FTP sites):

As I've said before, it appears that the great majority of players are male and the vast majority of them choose to present themselves as such. Some males, however, taking advantages of the relative rarity of females in MUDs, present themselves as female and thus stand out to some degree. Some use this distinction just for the fun of deceiving others, some of these going so far as to try to entice male-presenting players into sexually explicit discussions and interactions. This is such a widely noticed phenomenon, in fact, that one is advised by the common wisdom to assume that any flirtatious female-presenting players are, in real life, males. Such players are often subject to ostracism based on this assumption.

Curtis outlines the hurdles all this presents to authentic women who come online:

Female-presenting players report a number of problems. Many of them have told me that they are frequently subject both to harassment and to special treatment. One reported seeing two newcomers arrive at the same time, one male-presenting and one female-presenting. The other players in the room struck up conversations with the putative female and offered to show her around but completely ignored the putative male, who was left to his own devices.

In addition, probably due mostly to the number of female-presenting males one hears about, many female players report that they are frequently (and sometimes quite aggressively) challenged to "prove" that they are, in fact, female. To the best of my knowledge, male-presenting players are rarely if ever so challenged.

The issue of gender identity is often pointed up as one of the redeeming properties of the nets, but such an assumption, like all assumptions, has its doubters. The lack of physical presence may afford opportunity for the experimenters but generates confusion among others who wish for more certainty in their dealings. In fact, the issue of sex and gender can often seem like an albatross and unavoidable to the casual, non-sex-obsessed Net cruiser.

Rare is the night for the MUD-hopping traveler who doesn't have at least one conversation involving sex or gender. Part of it may be the overabundance of young adult males recently set loose (college students).

Hormone-drunk males—with no checks on their behavior and a certain amount of impunity in an uncensored atmosphere—can tend toward the sex-obsessed.

Laura Pace is working on a master's degree at the University of Southern California, the thesis for which will center on MUDS. "I think that, while admins of MUDs may be older, the 'typical' MUD player, if there is one, is probably between the ages of 16 and 22, and their mind-set, as often as not, is filled with gender confusion and raw porn. The availability of explicit sexual material on the Internet constantly amazes me, and if I can find it, the 16-year-old MUDder can certainly find it. The gender confusion is only exacerbated by the fact that, in MUDding, I have found it fairly typical that some mean-spirited person inaccurately represents his/her gender for the purposes either, I assume, of personal titillation or some sort of warped revenge mind-set. Therefore, MUDders tend to mistrust people until they are sure who they are in 'rl' [real life]. Although I am past the age where 'tinysex' [online descriptions of sexual interplay] or what have you, would be of interest, I think that many teenagers are seeking that sense of false intimacy and/or anonymous sexual discovery. It's the ultimate safe sex."

Consequences

It's a simple matter for a MUD administrator to identify and obliterate troublesome characters from their user roles, if they care to, and most do. Some do not. If a MUD administrator is particularly fearful that one or more disruptive types have been originating from the same host system, the entire system can be banned from the MUD.

Elizabeth Reid, in her article "Cultural Formations in Text-Based Virtual Realities," states:

> Gods and wizards may be the ultimate power within each MUD universe, and may often be the subject of respect and even fawning as players attempt to curry favor and gain privileges, but the atmosphere of respect which often surrounds them can lead to the favoring of players who are prepared to offer adulation, and passing over those who are not. The canny wielding of power

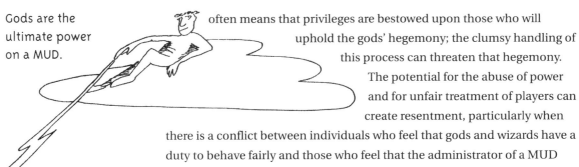

Gods are the ultimate power on a MUD.

often means that privileges are bestowed upon those who will uphold the gods' hegemony; the clumsy handling of this process can threaten that hegemony. The potential for the abuse of power and for unfair treatment of players can create resentment, particularly when there is a conflict between individuals who feel that gods and wizards have a duty to behave fairly and those who feel that the administrator of a MUD system has the right to do with it as he or she likes. The number of MUD systems in existence to some extent mitigates the potential for problems since, as one player replied, "look, it's his MUD, he can do what he wants. But if you don't like the MUD, don't play it!"

In-Character Behavior

On some systems, the question of character role-playing is not an issue, since the purpose of the MUD is merely to act as a gathering place. If there happens to be the accouterments of a fantasy or cyberpunk world, all the better. On other systems, though, the role-playing is the sole reason for existence.

Although there are rarely punishments for acting out-of-character, a serious role-playing MUD will have a heavy influence on even the casual visiting guest, carrying that player along with the theme.

P-Killing

Player killing is one in-character crime in many MUDs that will attract punishment from the wizards. In a small transference from real life, many MUDs frown upon p-killing or ban it outright, since resentment can be attached to losing your fantasy entity, which could lead to unpleasantness. Alternatively, there are MUDs in which the veteran players enjoy the prospect of newbie p-killing fodder.

On those systems where a rule against p-killing is in place, the punishment usually comes down from on high, with the player losing the

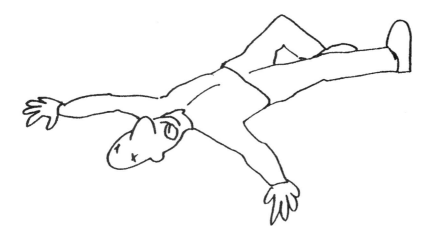

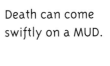
Death can come swiftly on a MUD.

character and the right to access. Some systems have less severe, but perhaps more humiliating, punishments, such as branding the character with a "scarlet letter" as a p-killer.

There is a movement afoot for devising methods that allow the players to police their own fantasy environments. GohsMUSH is one such place where great pains are being taken to portray a culture where penalties are swift and severe.

Geoff Tuffli is administrator of GohsMUSH. He and a character named Exeter (the author) met in a barroom in Gohs, an island city. Tuffli works a character named "Gohs" (the spelling of the following excerpt of an online conversation has been cleaned up and irrelevant passages excised):

```
Gohs says, "Shall we go elsewhere to avoid the periodic interrup-
tions of the ambiance system?"

Gohs steps out into the street.

Gohs has left.

Exeter steps out into the street.

Imperial Street

The flat gray stones of the street have been long-since worn
smooth by the countless passages of man and beast. Distantly, to
the north, you can see the inner gates of the city, and beyond
them, the Bridge of Flowers and the outer gates beyond even them,
while to the south the street widens and opens up into a vast
central plaza, where the tents of seemingly hundreds of merchants
cram the area, leaving little room for the common citizen.
```

Gohs moves off down the street, heading northwards.

Exeter makes his way up the street.

Imperial Street

The Imperial Street narrows slightly here in blatant contrast to
the broad thoroughfare to the north, where the caravan grounds on
the western side of the avenue crowd the roadway. Here, the
street is packed with merchants' shops and professional physi-
cians and alchemists of a hundred different kinds. To the north,
the blocky inner gates of the city rear up proudly over the
buildings, while to the south the street eventually opens up into
a broad central plaza. Eastwards a smaller, squarish plaza with a
lowered central area sits off the main road, silk-colored pavil-
ions lining the edges of the square.

Gohs walks into So'toa Plaza.

Exeter walks into So'toa Plaza.

So'toa Plaza

So'toa Plaza is only half as large as the huge central plaza, but
nonetheless it is nearly as well-frequented. It is the location
of the ritual gladiatorial games between denizens of the city and
the captured prisoners of the distant cities subjugated by Gohs.
Defeat may mean humiliation or death, but victory can bring
countless riches and wealth granted by the members of the Five
Houses to honor the brave of the city.

Gohs says, "There. That's good enough."

Exeter says, "So, is this a Moslem model? Turkic?"

Gohs says, "Closer to Aztec than anything else, but that's a
little deceptive. Religiously it's a cross between that, Japa-
nese, and Hindu. In other ways it's somewhat Persian or like
Constantinople. But if you assume a Turkic model, you won't go
too far wrong."

Exeter says, "Definitely different."

Gohs says, "One of the things I've wanted to do is to make sure
that if someone in character commits a crime, and is in-character
caught, he'll be in-character punished."

Exeter says, "What would constitute a crime, acting out-of-
character in the city? Talking about the Rolling Stones in the
Street of Dogs (whether it's appropriate or not)?"

Gohs says, "Oh, you mean crime in that sense."

Exeter says, "Well, I'm just trying to sort out what makes a
crime."

Gohs says, "When I refer to crime, I mean a character robbing
someone, murdering someone, blaspheming the gods, etc. That's all
in-character. If they do it and are caught in-characterly by the
city garrison, then they are punished in-character if they don't
escape or bribe their way out of it."

Gohs says, "If people are out-of-character in the streets, they'll simply have no excuse if a thug comes up and tries to mug them."

Gohs says, "I separate between in-character crimes and out-of-character violations of theme. For the latter, if it ever happens, the admin will just talk to the player and ask politely that they keep in-character.... For in-character crimes, that's no different than if you're in a role-playing game and your character in that robs some lady. Same thing."

Exeter says, "I just read the news law [the online help file outlining character punishment] and wondered what would draw such public 'canings' and such."

Exeter says, "Who will be enforcing? City guards? Will they be NPCs (Non-Player Characters)?"

Gohs says, "That sort of punishment is dealt with by the victim's relatives."

Gohs says, "City garrison are both players and NPCs, though the NPCs won't be able to guard against more of the laws than breaking up fights, probably."

Gohs says, "Depends on how well we can code them."

Gohs says, "If you actually get convicted of the crime and aren't released by the city garrison, which happens due to bribes and their own judgment, then you're usually executed. For things like assault, your family hires or itself exacts appropriate revenge (not including death, but virtually anything up to that is socially acceptable). This is good in another way, I think, because it encourages players to have their characters have relatives who are other players' characters."

Exeter says, "Do you see the players enforcing their own justice this way?"

Gohs says, "I think players will, yes."

Gohs says, "In fact, I suspect it'll get a bit out of hand, but that's the sort of thing that makes in-character role-playing more interesting. :-)"

Exeter says, "So you'll see little need of gods like yourself coming in to impose the law."

Gohs says, "May stimulate some laws to be passed by the Five Houses, etc."

Gohs says, "Administrators here upkeep the code, prevent things like harassment, maintain the site, and ensure to a reasonable standard that people stay at least roughly within theme, and that's more of a helping people to stay in theme rather than punishing them if they don't. Beyond that, admins aren't going to interfere with things. The admin won't be stepping in at all to enforce retribution or whatever. That's the players' job."

Gohs says, "We will arbitrate disputes if they arise, but so far there's been no need at all for that, and from my experiences elsewhere I think it'll be rare."

Gohs says, "I'm hoping it'll almost never be necessary except in the most extreme cases. In fact, a lot of the design for this place was to make it automated so as not to require the arbitration of a judge who may or may not be on and may or may not be disinterested and unbiased."

Exeter says, "Hm. So if a player calls the city guard, then the players playing the guards show up—or they don't—and enforce the law?"

Gohs says, "Right."

Gohs says, "The thing to keep in mind is that the city garrison's job is to keep the city stable and under control. In practice, they have a lot of latitude in how they do this. That's why it's up to them whether or not they actually prosecute someone. If they feel an example needs to be made, they do it, but if they think a stern reprimand will do the trick, they'll do that instead."

Exeter says, "Will there be theft allowed, of money and possessions?"

Gohs says, "Sure. Pick-pocketing code is almost done, in fact."

Gohs says, "And we already have ways of lock-picking doors and bashing them in."

Gohs says, "Since you can't lock possessions to yourself, if you're knocked unconscious, someone can steal them."

Exeter says, "And CAUGHT pick-pocketing code?"

Gohs says, "Yep. Depends on your skill, the lighting, and other sorts of things. "

Exeter says, "Will citizens be able to subdue each other?"

Gohs says, "You mean knock them unconscious?"

Exeter says, "Ah, and they stay unconscious for a random time, during which they can be moved and...stored?"

Gohs says, "Yes. Corpses, too, stay around. They rot, of course, but having them stay around allows for corpse-looting, funerals, putting them in the catacombs beneath the temple of Shaad-thi, that sort of thing."

Gohs says, "Being knocked unconscious unlocks you, and if the person trying to carry them is strong enough and isn't already carrying too much, they can pick up the character and tow them around."

Gohs says, "You can surrender and be manacled.... You can also be knocked unconscious, though it's better if you use a blunt object or your hands if you don't want to kill them. You've better chances then of knocking them out rather than killing them."

Attacks

The most ominous form of negative behavior involving MUDs is the growing threat posed by online vandals. These *crackers* (*hacker* is a misnomer) have shown up at the fringes of MUDdom, occasionally exploiting largely homegrown MUD software.

Lydia Leong, another maintainer of a MUD list and a World Wide Web page devoted to MUD information, posted "an open letter to a couple of self-proclaimed 'hackers'" on Usenet. The article put all on notice that the administrators and MUD community leaders were aware of threats to "bring down" dozens of MUDs on Halloween night, 1994.

Leong had indications that the attackers "wrote MUSHcode to systematically scan the database, object by object, for possibly vulnerable objects. The resulting list was then examined, one object at a time, for vulnerabilities."

Just the fact that admins became aware of the threat was a measure of defense in itself, although it's unfortunate that they had to divert effort away from the art of MUD creation and toward the task of defending against roving bands of marauding Net trashers.

One way of tightening up may be the trend toward registering all users. Many MUDs are wide open, but fewer than before. Many more are requiring full names and e-mail addresses, which could be used to trace vandals.

"Registration is pretty useful," says Leong. "The one remaining weakness is the possibility of using the guest character as a starting point for a denial-of-service attack (to use standard computer security jargon); this 'hole' is likely to be closed in server code (at least for MUSH) in the immediate future. Registration also doesn't eliminate the possibility of being attacked by a disgruntled player, but the fact that one does have e-mail addresses on hand makes this fairly unlikely.

"The incident which comes to mind is an attack on PernMUSH and SouCon MUSH some years ago, by a disgruntled ex-player. He had been reading the server coder's mailing list, which [was] open to any who [wished] to subscribe. I had posted about a bug which could be used to freeze the games for long periods of time; he logged onto both MUSHes and typed the command to trigger that bug repeatedly.

"While the games were down for the code upgrade to patch the bug, the site admin for PernMUSH and SouCon posted a message on the game's usual addresses, explaining what had happened and posting the e-mail address of the offending player, encouraging players to express their displeasure to him directly. The results were predictable."

Leong expects to provide automated tools to test MUSH security at some point in the future, and presumably similar tools are in development for all the other MUD flavors. According to Leong, there were no reported MUD trashings on Halloween 1994.

Nonetheless, just as residents of Detroit, Michigan, and Camden, New Jersey, can count on the annual Mischief Night arson sprees, so too might we expect that Halloween becomes an annual occasion for threats of online "arson"—this time by the overprivileged techno-geeks with a bit too much access to the greatest communication tool yet devised: a free and open international computer web.

Chapter 5

Practical MUDding

Getting There

The initial task in assuring immediate (and enduring) enjoyment of the interactive networking experience is to scout the environment wisely. Individual MUDs may come and go, but you will always happen upon at least one, and probably many more, to which you will return often. Here friendships will develop, insofar as online friendships can. At the least, you may search out and find a group of MUDders who are merely mildly annoying. Finding them really isn't difficult. Just start at your host system.

Gopher

Your MUD prospecting may begin with the aptly named *gopher*—the burrowing Internet search facility—if your host system includes MUD as a choice of direction for the rodent to dig.

Delphi Internet's gopher has a facility for accessing MUDs directly. To get there, go to the Internet area and type:

```
gopher
```

Here's what you'll see:

```
Type HELP for a list of commands
Internet SIG Gopher
Page 1 of 1

1    PERSONAL FAVORITES                                     Menu
2    "ABOUT DELPHI'S GOPHER SERVICE"                        Text
3    *** FAQ: FREQUENTLY ASKED QUESTIONS *** (REVISED 11/4)    Menu
4    ALL THE WORLD'S GOPHERS                                Menu
5    BUSINESS AND ECONOMICS                                 Menu
6    COMPUTERS                                              Menu
7    FREE-NETS AND COMMUNITY ACCESS                         Menu
8    FTP: DOWNLOADABLE PROGRAMS, IMAGES, SOUNDS             Menu
9    GAMES AND MUDS, MUSHES, MUSES, AND MOOS                Menu
10   GOVERNMENT AND POLITICS                                Menu
11   HEALTH AND MEDICINE                                    Menu
12   INTERNET INFORMATION                                   Menu
13   LAW                                                    Menu
14   LIBRARIES AND RESEARCH GUIDES                          Menu
15   SCHOOLHOUSE (K-12)                                     Menu
16   SEARCH UTILITIES                                       Menu
17   SUBJECT MATTER MENUS                                   Menu
18   THE GRAB BAG (WITH WHAT'S NEW 11/23)                   Menu
19   WORLD WIDE WEB                                         Menu
Enter Item Number,?, or EXIT:
```

Among all the other network sites to which the gopher might take you, you'll see the selection for MUDs. Type the number for your selection:

```
9
```

Another menu scrolls up:

```
GAMES AND MUDS, MUSHES, MUSES, AND MOOS
1    Backgammon Server                                      Telnet
2    Chess Connections                                      Menu
3    The Games Domain (web links to game information)        WWW/Web
4    Go Server                                              Telnet
5    Hunt!  A multi-player multi-terminal game.             Telnet
6    Othello Server                                         Telnet
7    READ, if you have display problems                     Text
8    MUDs, MUSHes, MUSEs, and MOOs                          Text
9    The following two items are both based on Doran's MUDlist.
     If you don't see what you want in one, try the other, since
     either one may be more up to date than the other.       Text
10   CONNECT to MUDs (all types)                            Menu
11   Tarp3's Web Access to MUDs                             WWW/Web
12   Doran's MUDlist, 10/15                                 Text
13   MUD Announcements (rec.games.mud.announce)             Usenet
14   Lydia Leong's MUD Resources                            WWW/Web
15   Aragorn server                                         WWW/Web
16   Mother Gopher's MUDlist (U of Minn)                    Menu
Enter Item Number, MORE, ?, or BACK:
```

Along with other game sites, you'll see a cornucopia of MUD resources, including access to Usenet conferences on the subject, FAQs, and lists. On the left is the selection number, on the right is the description of the resources to be accessed. A menu will open up another level of choices.

Type:

```
13
```

The result:

```
CONNECT to MUDs (all types)
Page 1 of 31

1    Use the FIND command to look for MUDs by name or type  Text
2    TYPE aber: An old hack and slash style mud.            Text
3    BabeMUD                                                Telnet
4    BernieMUD                                              Telnet
5    Budapest                                               Telnet
6    DragonMud                                              Telnet
7    Eclipse MUD                                            Telnet
8    Infinity                                               Telnet
9    Kender's Kove                                          Telnet
10   Mustang                                                Telnet
11   Northern Lights                                        Telnet
12   PuRgAtorY                                              Telnet
13   Rainbow                                                Telnet
14   Silver                                                 Telnet
15   Sleepless Nights                                       Telnet
16   Terradome                                              Telnet
17   Tyrann II                                              Telnet
Enter Item Number, MORE, SAVE, ?, or BACK: 12
```

This is the first of 31 pages (screens) full of listings that will offer to link you directly to the entryways of the named MUDs. The column on the right indicates that telnet will access the resources for you, so there's no need even to type in the MUD's address. In fact, if all your MUDding is accomplished in this way, you may never need to know the address at all.

Typing

```
12
```

will take you directly to *Northern Lights*, an AberMUD.

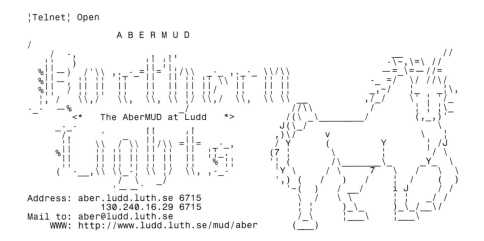

```
¦Telnet¦ Open
                A B E R M U D
```

Address: aber.ludd.luth.se 6715
         130.240.16.29 6715
Mail to: aber@ludd.luth.se
    WWW: http://www.ludd.luth.se/mud/aber

MUDserver

Though it won't connect you directly, another resource for finding the
addresses of MUDs is the MUDserver, a list of MUD addresses with search
capabilities maintained by one "Howard." At your telnet prompt, type:

```
bob.coe.uga.edu 4801
```

This is what you'll see:

```
                    Welcome to the AUTOMATED MUDLIST.
Type QUIT in all CAPS to exit this server.
Type @mudlist NAME for a listing  of MUDs.  Wild cards
are acceptable.  Submissions and corrections MUST be in
this format: PORT IP _ADDRESS HOST_ADDRESS TYPE NAME
Type help for more info.

Typing help gives the commands:

Examples:
    @mudlist After    (Lists out MUDS that start with "After")
    @mudlist A*Five   (Lists out MUDS that start with "A" and
end with "Five")
    @mudlist Sa*      (Lists out MUDS that start with "Sa")
    @mudlist *Land*   (Lists out MUDS that have "Land" in their
name)
```

So, if you were looking for all the MUDs out there with *moo* in their names,
making them likely sites for MOO-type environments, you would type:

```
@mudlist *moo*
```

This use of the "wild card" asterisks searches for all occurrences of *moo* anywhere in a name. The resulting list may look like this:

```
MUD NAME              IP ADDRESS        HOST NAME
PORT                  STATUS            TYPE
###################################################################

MirrorMOO             129.10.112.76     mirror.ccs.neu.edu
8889                  UNKNOWN           dgd
_____

MooseHead Mud         204.122.16.44     mud.eskimo.com
4000                  UNKNOWN           diku
_____

Moonstar              192.135.84.5      pulsar.hsc.edu
4321                  UNKNOWN           lp
_____

Newmoon               131.252.21.12     jove.cs.pdx.edu
7680                  UNKNOWN           lp
_____

BayMOO                165.113.1.30      mud.crl.com
8888                  UNKNOWN           moo
_____

DreamMOO              192.245.137.1     Feenix.metronet.com
8888                  UNKNOWN           moo
_____

Final Frontiers MOO   192.204.120.2     ugly.microserve.net
2499                  UNKNOWN           moo
_____

LambdaMOO             192.216.54.2      lambda.xerox.com
8888                  UNKNOWN           moo
_____

MediaMOO              18.85.0.48        purple-crayon.media.mit.edu
8888                  UNKNOWN           moo
_____

MuMOO                 192.94.216.74     chestnut.enmu.edu
7777                  UNKNOWN           moo
_____

NovaMOO/AM            199.217.152.5     hades.inlink.com
5000                  UNKNOWN           moo
_____
```

```
StarMOO                192.217.232.8        asimov.elk-
grove.k12.il.us
6879                   UNKNOWN              moo

TrekMOO                192.204.120.2        trekmoo.microserve.com
2499                   UNKNOWN              moo

ValhallaMOO            192.55.87.211        valhalla.acusd.edu
4444                   UNKNOWN              moo
```

The list gives each MUD's name, its nominal and numerical address, and its type. In this case, the status of each MUD is listed as "unknown" because at the time of this writing, that feature was disabled; as a result, all statuses were listed as "unknown." This does not mean the MUDs were down. Nor does it mean they were up. Their status was just that, unknown.

The search above indeed came up with several MOO-type environments, as well as MUDs with *moo* in the name.

To leave the server, type:

```
QUIT
```

Other Sources

The number one "other source" is the appendix in the back of this book. It lists most of the MUDs in existence at the time of this writing. Also, look around online for the Yanoff list, the Big Fun list, and the December list, all of which contain information on MUDs and many other facets of the networked universe.

Being There

Registration

Some sites make it easier to join than others. The trend these days is toward *registration*, which refers to the sending of "real-life" information to the MUD system (the operators of which are not, in every case, too forthcoming with their own information). The rise in attacks by Net trolls and vandals has led to these tightened security measures.

Caution in this area is understandable, and home phone numbers and addresses should not be shared with unknown system operators, especially those at sites with not-readily-identifiable "business" offices. Your online service will have your address and should keep it in confidence. The few MUDs on the Net that require payment will, for obvious reasons, require billing information. For most MUDs, however, your name and e-mail address should be sufficient.

Most people in everyday life are fairly free with such sensitive information. Think of the photo developing service at your supermarket, or your local dry cleaner. They have your address and phone number. How well do you know them? Fortunately, instances of abuse are almost as rare on the Internet as they are at the corner store.

Caution is warranted, however. The best advice is not to give out any information unless the receiver is traceable and your level of confidence in the recipient high. If you're not sure, don't give it out.

Perhaps the majority of systems still require no ID. Whether it's because they have more airtight security, more diligent oversight, or merely rely on their ability to trace users to host systems (which *is* possible), these open sites require nothing more than that a player appear at the "door" and name a character.

Most MUDs provide clear instructions on registering characters in their opening screens. Sometimes the opening screens also state how to come in as a guest. Once inside, use the **help** command, which is honored nearly universally. Type:

```
help register
```

or:

```
help new
```

or something similar, and text instructions will likely follow. If not, see the next section on how to list all the commands the MUD has available.

Command Lists

The huge number of varying MUD systems precludes any comprehensive listing of individual commands. This section will address, in a generalized fashion, the major commands that are common to nearly all systems. Individual syntax (the rules governing the commands usage) may vary, but not really that much. The beauty of the MUD world is that, since the environments were always open to a networking public of varying technical prowess, the commands are necessarily intuitive and simple. Once experienced with the possibilities of syntax, you'll soon find it possible to guess what to do, even on a strange system or when faced with a MUD variation never before seen. And since their roots lie partially in the world of interactive fiction, MUD commands are, in nearly every case, *descriptive* of the actions intended. So, if you want to get something and you're on a MUD for the first time, more than likely just typing *get* and then the name of that object will work. Or try *get all*. This will get you that object and any others that may be lying around the room.

The online help facilities on MUDs are invaluable in sorting out the correct way to execute actions. And surprisingly—for a discipline of computing with very little in the way of, well, discipline—online help files in MUDS range from very good to excellent.

Help

Nearly every MUD, MOO, MUSH and/or MUCK, if not *all* network sites and systems, supply some form of online help. Usually this is accessible by just typing:

```
help
```

Typing **help** and the command or topic on which help is needed will result in a text explanation of that command or topic.

Type:

```
help commands
```

and a list of all commands may appear.

Sometimes merely typing:

```
commands
```

will also result in a list of commands.

Typing **help** at the *Northern Lights* AberMUD will produce this screen:

```
Some Standard Commands, there are plenty of others....
-=-=-=-=-=-=-=-=-=-=-=-=-=-=-=-=-=-=-=-=-=-=-=-=-=-=-=-=-=-=-=-=-
Moving Around              | Communication
  N  E  S  W  U  D      STAND   JUMP  | SAY      SHOUT      TELL     TELLBACK
  LOOK       EXITS   SIT     SLEEP | WISH     MAIL       BACKOFF  NOREMOTE
  AUTOEXITS                 |
-=-=-=-=-=-=-=-=-=-=-=-=-=-=-=-=-=-=-=-=-=-=-=-=-=-=-=-=-=-=-=-=-
Items                     | Informational
  GET      DROP    WEAR    REMOVE | SCORE    VALUE      LEVELS   COUPLES
  GIVE     STEAL   INVEN   PUT    | HELP     INFO       WHO      QUESTS
  EXAMINE  LIGHT   UNLIGHT PLAY   | VERSION  CREDITS    PN       QLIST
  PUSH     TURN    OPEN    CLOSE  | WIZLIST  ACTIONS    BULLETIN QDONE
  LOCK     UNLOCK  EAT     EMPTY  | USERS    IUSERS     MUSERS   TIME
  REPAIR   THROW   RUB            |
-=-=-=-=-=-=-=-=-=-=-=-=-=-=-=-=-=-=-=-=-=-=-=-=-=-=-=-=-=-=-=-=-
Combat          | Magic      | Utility
  KILL   WIELD  | SPELLS     | !        BUG        BECOME   CFR
  FLEE   WIMPY  |            | CLS      COLOR      NOMOTD   PLINES
                |            | QUIET    SAVE       SUGGEST  TYPO
                |            | ASSIST                       QUIT
-=-=-=-=-=-=-=-=-=-=-=-=-=-=-=-=-=-=-=-=-=-=-=-=-=-=-=-=-=-=-=-=-
Type HELP <command> for detailed help on a command.
```

Consult your system or terminal program documentation to find out how you can **capture** or **log** this help text to a file as it scrolls up the screen. If you intend to spend time on a particular MUD or type of MUD, making your own guidebook from the screen readouts—or at least posting a print-out of commands on your wall—will help you learn the ropes in the early stages and can serve as an easy reference later.

Interactive Help

Sometimes a MUD will have a wizard or an advanced player or two hanging around to help newcomers. In spite of the Net's reputation for inhospitality, there are many MUDs in which folks do volunteer to help.

Some even offer automated tours, like this one at the *MUD II* on IPlay, a commercial Interneted service.

Once inside the MUD, type:

```
guestify
```

Then type:

```
tour1
```

Text will scroll up your screen as the system takes you on an automated tour of the sights most amenable to new players:

```
Starting tour 1 of the cottage.
You are now Murgatroyd the touring guest.
You have suddenly and magically started glowing!
Path.
You are standing on a path which leads off a road to the north,
to a cottage south of you. To the west and east are separate
gardens.
*It has started to rain.
*[OK, this is the entrance to the cottage, which is one of the
best places for novices to go as it generally has a lot of
novice-grade treasure ("trinkets") lying around in it. Just to
make it even easier, you'll notice it doesn't even have a front
door. It's not a difficult place to find. Simply wander along the
road until you stumble across it.]
*[We're going south.]
```

Some players will also offer to help you. More often than not, you'll encounter a helpful co-adventurer willing to give a few tips. Online, as in real life, people are looking for allies—and like to show off their special knowledge.

Categorical Commands

There are three areas in which commands may be categorized. In the sections that follow, we'll look at some common commands and concepts in these three areas: navigation, communication, and objectives.

Navigation Commands

To get from place to place, one must navigate.

Neswud

The letters above represent the standard text "direction compass" available in most situations. No need to type:

```
North
```

Just type:

```
n
```

It follows then that **e** is east, **s** is south, **w** is west, **u** is up and **d** is down.

Often the in-between points on the compass are represented as well, so that **nw** is northwest, **ne** is northeast, **sw** is southwest and **se** is southeast.

Exits

Some MUDs have more descriptive commands for moving from area to area. For instance, on *MUD II* at IPlay, if you enter the first area—with the **auto exits** feature active—the system will tell you where you can go from wherever you are. For example:

```
The Village Green
You are standing on a square of grass in the center of the
village.  A road leads east into the rest of the village.
To the north is a small church, and a path leads west into the
trees.
The sky is covered by a thick layer of clouds.
An old spear lies here on the ground.

Obvious exits are:
North : The Village Church
East  : Village Track
South : Rough Land
West  : The Humpbacked Bridge
```

Many MUDs provide this type of information by default, offering a command to shut them off and showing these exits only when an **exits** command is invoked.

At times, though, as in *MUD II*, the exit names will be simple directions, with more descriptive places attached.

For example, when leaving the Elizabethan tea room on *MUD II* at IPlay (the room where all logons begin), this is what you'd see:

Tip: Every time you sip tea in the tea room, your starting point will change.

```
As you step through the opening, you become swathed in a fine,
gossamer mist. The Elizabethan tea room fades hazily away, and
vague, new shapes begin to form around you. Their outlines become
more defined, their colors grow stronger, and the mist thins out
into pale wisps, which gradually disperse away to nothingness....

Badly paved road.
You find yourself on a badly paved road, which continues to the
east and west. North and northeast are the lower regions of a
mountain, which rises up beyond the clouds. Southeast is a yard,
belonging to an inn which can be seen just beyond it. South is a
briar patch, and southwest the foothills of a more impressive
mountain. Northwest is a deep valley, whose western slopes rise up
to the foothills of a mountain more majestic still. The view is
quite breathtaking. It is raining.

    up:             Middle mountain.
    in:             Valley between mountains.
    out:            Badly paved road.
    swampward:      Foothills.
    southwest:      Foothills.
    south:          Briar patch.
    southeast:      Side yard of inn.
    northeast:      Middle mountain.
    northwest:      Valley between mountains.
    west:           Badly paved road.
    east:           Badly paved road.
    north:          Middle mountain.
```

At times, there are more elaborate navigation aids available, as illustrated by this short trip in Ragnarok:

```
You are in the house of the Bonder Sverre, at the Crossroads
of the World. There is a door in the west wall. There is a
button beside the door. You can see a room to the northeast
that glitters with candlelight. Another room is to the southeast
that has lots of people in white uniforms running around. There
is an exit to the south, southeast, north, northeast and west.

>E

Going East

Windswept plain
You are on a windswept muddy plain south of the Crossroads.
You are standing in yellow-gray mud, in a narrow track no more than
```

```
two feet wide. On either side the gray-green of dying grass
begins.
You can see a road farther to the east.
There are three obvious exits: north, west, and east.
There is a sign here, by the side of the track.
To the south you see a shimmering in the air, and the
words "Welcome Ye Newe Adventurer!" glimmer for a moment
and then wink out.
Perhaps you can go south, and others can't?
It's a clear, cold winter afternoon.
There a hole in the ground here.
A tall wooden post stands here with arrows pointing off in
various directions. There is writing on the flat wooden arrows:
    Post Office:          eess.
    Adventurer's Guild:   eees.
    Shop:                 eeen.
    Pub:                  eene.
    Lockers:              eenn.
    Bank of Alphasia:     eeeennw.
    Two Goats Antiques:   eeeenne.
```

This signpost gives directions to various locations of interest to a new adventurer. Typing **e**, **e**, **n**, and **e**, then, should take us to that pub:

```
>e

Village track
A muddy track going into the village. The track opens
up to a road to the east and ends with a windswept plain
to the west. There is a gravel road to the south.
There are three obvious exits: west, east, and south.

>e

The Ragnarok Library. A sign on the door says, 'CLOSED.'

>n

Small yard
A small yard surrounded by houses. There is a pub to the east, a
newspaper station to the west and a locker rental shop to the
north.
There are four obvious exits: south, east, west, and north.

>e

You are in the local pub, a cheerful place with many long
wooden benches and stained tables. A breeze blows through the
open windows, making the lantern flames flicker and dance. There
is a sign on the counter.
```

```
You can buy drinks here.
We have the following drinks:

    First class beer    : 12
    Mountain Dew         : 38
    Special of the house : 151
    Firebreather         : 540
```

Communication Commands

The next major category of commands involves making your character speak. Most MUDs adhere to a sort of *sound perspective*, in that the textual environment—what is sometimes pretentiously termed the *spatial metaphor*—will dictate not only how a location "looks" in terms of text descriptives, but also how it "sounds" in terms of determining whose computer screens reflect which utterances.

Broadly, no matter which system you are projected to, there will be:

- Ways to talk to just one person at a time (**tell** or **whisper**)

- Methods for talking to everyone in a room in which you are present (**say**)

- Ways to talk to everyone in the whole MUD (**shout**)

- Some special communication modes that vary more severely from system to system, concerning *chat* channels and MUD *mail*.

Say

Say is the basic common form of communication. With it, you can talk to a gathering of people in the same room or location. For instance, typing:

```
say The max is blue.
```

will result in a message on your screen like this:

```
You say, "The max is blue."
```

Others present in the room will see something like this:

```
George says, "The max is blue."
```

On the vast majority of systems, typing the three-letter sequence

S-A-Y, chore that it is, can be replaced simply by typing a single key, normally the double quotes:

"

So if you typed **"the max is blue** (ending quotes not normally required) the result would be the same as above. The shortcut will become second nature and eventually the only way you say anything.

Tell or Whisper

When you want to speak with only one person, usually in the same room but sometimes in a distant part of the MUD, many systems (but not all) support a **tell** and/or **whisper** command. The form is normally:

```
tell somecharactername something
```

If you typed:

```
tell Ursula I love you.
```

The result on your screen would be:

```
You tell Ursula "I love you."
```

Ursula's screen would print:

```
George tells you, "I love you."
```

or something similar.

No one else in the room would hear the comment, except, of course, wizards with the power to hear all.

On some systems it's not necessary to type the word **tell**. Just typing

```
Ursula I love you.
```

will accomplish the same thing.

The **whisper** command works the same way as **tell** when it is available.

Page

Page is another variation of **tell**, the difference being that on some systems **page** is the "**shout** form of **tell**." You can **page** a message to a user in some other part of the environment.

Shout

The **shout** command on most systems allows you to say something to every character in the MUD. Be warned, though: most MUD communities frown on excessive shouting, and some would rather not have any. **Shout** works the same way as **say**, normally with the messages being carried to the screen of every person logged into the MUD.

For instance, if you typed:

```
shout James wants me dead.
```

everyone in the MUD would see

```
George shouts, "James wants me dead."
```

On some systems, the source of the shout will be identified only to those in the same immediate area, who would likely see the shouter. Others would see something like:

```
Someone shouts, "James wants me dead."
```

Mail and Chat

MUDmail varies greatly in its availability. Some systems have extensive mail subsystems. Others don't bother at all. Look around for it, as it can be useful for leaving notes to friends (or enemies) who are not online at the same time as you.

It may seem silly, or at best redundant, for a MUD to have chat channels within it, since that's what the whole system appears to be designed for—chatting. But often, internal MUD chat channels (sometimes called *chats* or *channels*) are theme-oriented. For instance, on a cyberpunk-themed MUD like *Nuclear War*, there are "radio" channels available which are named according to frequencies to which a player can tune his or her character's radio.

In either of these features, mail or chat, the MUD will have help files describing how they are used.

In MUDs, not only can you "say" things with the commands listed above, but you can *do* things, as well.

Emote

This command is most often used to make your character perform some action of your choosing. It takes the form:

```
emote someaction
```

where **someaction** is anything you want to do. For example, typing:

```
emote stands on his head.
```

would result in the message:

```
you stands on his head.
```

Everyone else in the room would see:

```
George stands on his head.
```

It's important that the typer form actions in the third person, even though the message sent back to the source may be ungrammatical. Remember your audience.

Emoting can be used to express nonverbal information, gestures, and motion. It can also be used to create a sort of thought balloon form of verbal phrasing, as opposed to "out loud" dialogue. So typing:

```
emote rights himself and wonders what came over him.
```

would result in the outgoing message:

```
George rights himself and wonders what came over him.
```

The shorthand form of **emote** is almost universally the colon (:). No space is normally necessary after the colon. Thus, typing:

```
:bends over red-faced and begins to pick up his change.
```

would result in the outgoing message:

```
George bends over red-faced and begins to pick up his change.
```

Some systems offer a variety of preset "emotes" that work the same for everyone. For common actions, these commands serve to save keystrokes, enhance the atmosphere with easily invoked actions, and also improve the overall level of spelling in the environment.

Typing **help action** on an AberMUD, then, might reveal a huge list of "canned" actions, such a this one:

```
Accuse   Aguitar  Apology  Applaud  Argh      Arm      Arrest   Aww      Backrub
Bark     Bashful  Bearhug  Beam     Beer      Beg      Bite     Blam     Blanket
Blink    Blowk    Blush    Bomb     Boot      Bop      Bored    Bounce   Bow
Brb      Bucket   Burp     Cackle   Caress    Censor   Cheer    Chuckle  Clap
Comb     Comfort  Confuse  Congrat  Content   Cool     Cough    Cringe   Cross
Cry      Csaw     Cuddle   Curtsey  Cutfry    Dance    Dika     Drool    Dsnort
Eblow    Eek      Embrace  Envy     Evil      Excited  Fart     Faint    Finger
Flex     Flip     Flame    Fnord    French    Frown    Fruit    Gasp     Giggle
Glare    Goodnit  Goose    Greet    Grin      Grit     Groan    Growl    Grumble
Hand     Happy    Headb    Hiccup   Hifive    Hmm      Hold     Howl     Hum
Hypno    Ibb      Incline  Innoc    Kick      Kneel    Knurd    Koosh    Kvetch
Lag      Late     Laugh    Lip      Listen    Love     Martian  Massage  Moan
Moose    Mumble   Neck     Nibble   Nod       Nosepat  Nudge    Nuzzle   Onion
Panic    Pant     Peer     Pinch    Pine      Ping     Poke     Ponder   Pounce
Pout     Proud    Puke     Punch    Purr      Raindan  Raise    Relief   Rofl
Rose     Ruffle   Salute   Scare    Schmoo    Scratch  Scream   Shake    Sheesh
Shiver   Shoe     Shrug    Shun     Sigh      Slap     Smile    Smirk    Smooch
Snap     Sneer    Sneeze   Snicker  Sniff     Sniffle  Snore    Snort    Snowb
Snuggle  Sob      Spank    Spit     Squeeze   Stare    Stomp    Strip    Strut
Sulk     Sundanc  Swallow  Tantrum  Tap       Taunt    Tea      Tease    Thank
Toe      Tohappy  Tongue   Trust    Tweak     Twiddle  Tyger    Violin   Waltz
Warcry   Whew     Whimper  Whine    Whistle   Wiggle   Wink     Worship  Worthy
Yawn     Yodel    Yy       Dive     Flowers   Hug      Kiss     Lick     Meditat
Pet      Pray     Rub      Sing     Think     Tickle   Wave
```

So if you type:

```
puke
```

you would see the message:

```
You puke on your shoes.
```

The rest of the room would see:

```
George pukes on his shoes.
```

If you type:

```
yodel
```

you'll see:

```
You yodel your lungs off.
```

and everyone else will see:

```
George yodels his lungs off.
```

If you type:

```
sneeze
```

you'll see:

```
Gesundheit!
```

and the rest of the room will see:

```
George sneezes.
```

Goals

Experience points are normally earned in the process of achieving higher "levels" for your character. At the lower levels, the goal most often is to survive. At certain higher levels, the goal may be to achieve the status of wizard.

Your online presence can have characteristics that vary according to a select set of *races* or *classes*. *Race* refers more to the concepts and traditions of fantasy literature "species" than to what the word implies in the real world. Some choices of race could include human, dwarf, or elf.

Class refers to the aptitude of the character, which usually reflects the player's desire to go about the game in a certain style. Two major classes are *fighter* and *magic user*. These two have many subcategories. The basic difference between them is that the warriors smash their way through obstacles, and sorcerers try to survive by their wiles and spells.

Check the rules concerning level attainment and character class/race for the MUDs you like most. The possibilities vary greatly.

Experience points can be earned by collecting treasure or defeating monsters (often referred to as *mobiles*). Sometimes there are quests to complete.

Commands for fighting include the intuitive, such as **hit**, **kill**, **smite**, or **strike**. No need to elaborate. **Spells** are also available for characters of the correct type and high level. These may do damage to enemies or heal friends and/or oneself.

The higher-level wizards are often rewarded with a *builder bit*, sometimes called a *wizard bit*. This is a setting in the character file of the MUD's database that allows the player, through the actions of the character, to add features or areas to the MUD or otherwise change the environment.

In noncompetitive, so-called "social" MUDs, there is no treasure gathering, fighting, defeating, or questing. The goals may have less to do with competing than with communicating and connecting. On these systems, too, the environment can be built and changed, most notably on the MOO-based systems. The basic programming required for this will be outlined in a later chapter.

Walk Through

The following actual episode took place in *Northern Lights*. Though this passage has no fighting, many of the above-mentioned commands and principles do make appearances. The incident illustrates the value of friendliness, as well as the amount of help that can be had from fellow MUDders.

```
                        Welcome To Northern Lights

     The Hallway
     You stand in a long, dark hallway, which echoes to the tread of
     your booted feet. You stride on down the hall, choose your
     masque, and enter the worlds beyond the known....

     Entering Game... Welcome, Vince Clortho!

     The Northern Lights Welcome Centre
     You are standing in a large room, covered with pictures of the
     sights
     from around the MUD. One large sign states, 'Welcome to Northern
     Lights!'
     If you are new to AberMUDs, or to MUDs in general, you might wish
     to go
     through our guided tour. If you don't wish to take the tour, you
     can go
     west to the temple, or south to the village church. A door opens
     up to
     a clearing to the east, where your guide is waiting patiently.
        To start the tour, type "E."
```

(Here's the tour.)

```
     A receptionist sits behind a desk in the corner, smiling at you.

     >e
     >The Start of the Tour
```

```
You find yourself in a clearing in a forest. This is where the
tour
starts. An open door leads back to the welcome centre and a broad
path leads off to the east, but you feel unsure of how you are
going to get
there.
A large sign has been nailed to a tree.
It is raining.
Your Guide is sitting on a stone, waiting for you to read the
sign by the path.
```

(Real players begin to speak.)

```
Rob tells you 'hello!'  (A tell.)
Grock appears with an ear-splitting bang.
>You say 'hiya'  (A say.)
Grock says 'hiya'
Grock smiles happily.  (The smile action.)
Grock says 'If you need any help, just ask.'
Grock bows gracefully.  (Another action, bow.)
>You say 'thanks.'
Rob tells you 'what's up?'  (A tell.)
>You tell Rob 'not much. How bout you?'
Rob tells you 'nothing really.'
>You say 'so it goes.'
Grock says 'vince clortho... what's that from?'
Grock says 'yes, so it goes.'  (Sometimes the lag factor can cause
conversations to become a bit disjointed.)
```

```
>You tell Grock 'ah. You know the name. Good.'
>You say 'Ghostbusters.'
Phenix shouts 'bye, all'  (A shout.)
Grock says 'oh, that's right.'
Grock says 'the Key Master.'
It has started to rain.  (Some systems "simulate" weather.)
>You say 'Yah, the key master.'
Grock says 'I am vince clortho, key master of gozer.'
Grock says 'gozer the gozerian.'
>You say 'ha ha.'
Grock says 'are you the gate keeper?'
Grock becomes the Gate Keeper.  (An emote.)
>You say 'Is there room enough for both of us in there?'
Grock falls down laughing.
Grock says 'so, she sleeps above her covers.'
>You say 'hyuk.'
Grock says 'Four FEET above her covers.'
>You say 'heh, heh.'
Grock says 'have you abered before?'
>You say 'nope, first time. What goes on?'
Grock says 'well, mostly you do quests.'
Bonkers has arrived.  (Another player enters the area.)
Bonkers has gone north.  (Then exits north.)
Rob tells you 'wanna get to level 3 real fast?'  (An offer of a
shortcut from level one to three.)
```

```
>you say, 'sure.'
>exits  (Checking to see the exits.)
>Obvious exits are:
North : End of Gap
South : Dark Tunnel

Rob says, 'follow me.'
Rob goes south.
>s
>you go south

Dark Tunnel
You are following a dim, magically lit tunnel which burrows deep
underground.
The walls glow gently, showing off the myriad sparkling colors of
the tunnel walls, which were quite evidently dug, and are cer-
tainly not natural.
```

And you're off.

Chapter 6

An IRC User's Manual

for those who see the room descriptions and other *spatial meta–phor* trappings of MUDs as unnecessary hindrances to their *chatability*, for those who want the purest real-time capabilities of this global, interwebbed bitstream, there's the raw conversation channels of the *Internet Relay Chat*—the infamous IRC.

The reader may come to this section with some preconceived notions about IRC, built on rumor, mainstream media ignorance, hearsay, and perhaps some personal experience. This bad reputation is, to a limited extent, deserved. According to Bruce Sterling in his electronic update to *The Hacker Crackdown*, IRC is where all the phone freaks and crackers now reside.

In IRC, an anarchist's dream, there are almost no rules, and though there are still more or less half-hearted hierarchies of control, the atmosphere of pure freedom is palpable. And so the drawbacks of such undistilled freedom also hit the unprepared user square in the face. If you ever wanted a taste of what the world would be like with no social checks and balances, drop in on IRC. Here be chaos.

Graffiti, Loud Radios

For those who have never been there, several words of caution are in order. Some information here can prevent damage to your computer. Some can prevent damage to your ego.

Before getting into the commands used in the IRC morass, there is one command that we can discuss early. This is the /**kick** command. Simply put, /**kick** can be used by anyone on a channel who holds the *channel operator* powers. This title can be passed from user to user, and certain users can wield the /**kick** command like a sword.

There may be times you see yourself kicked for simply mistyping. You may get kicked by an "official" authority figure for suspected hacking (no due process here), or for being a user who is accessing IRC from a disapproved host system ("**kick** No Delphi Internet users allowed here. **kick**"), or for no particular or identifiable reason at all.

There's no need to be upset, or pursue redress. It's too minor an affront for any overseeing *IRC Operator,* or *IRCop,* to get involved. Move on to friendlier or more compatible channels. There are plenty—thousands, in fact.

These same kicking and screaming networkers would likely be painting graffiti or driving with ear-splitting car radios as their modes of power projection in real life. At least while they're on IRC, we can take solace that their physical presence is far from ours.

Protect Yourself

On IRC you rub elbows with the hordes of anarchist posers and hangers-on and possibly the occasional genuine article. There are software pirates and pornography disseminators, vandals, Beavis-and-Butthead soundalikes, and the occasional genuinely defective unit. For the most part, there is no danger. As in any community, if you fall in with the wrong crowd and follow the direction of those not to be trusted, trouble can result.

If someone takes a disliking to you, there's also the possibility they may attempt to *flood* your system with a stream of text, sometimes obscenity-laden. This is rare and will sometimes overload other computer systems on the Net as well. There are deterrents to this behavior, since IRC operators regard it as a serious misuse (as opposed to wrongful **/kick**ing, which isn't generally regarded as an offense or investigated). These IRC overlords, when aroused, have the means for tracking down offenders (the Net is not completely anonymous, as is generally believed). If it occurs, generally it's best just to avoid channels with your nemesis in the future. If there's a persistent problem, then report it to your local system administrator. Resist complaining to an IRCop unless drastic measures are called for, because this complaint would be just that.

Why Bother?

None of the above is to say that IRC cannot be fun or useful. There's no easier way to set up a channel for discussions with associates spread out across the globe at negligible cost (compared to, say, the cost of an international conference call that lasts for hours). But a few precautions may help prevent a wide range of unpleasantness:

- Don't give out any information where strangers can overhear. The best way to accomplish this is to *never give out any personal information on the Net at any time*. This includes password information, your address, and phone numbers. The reasons for this are obvious. It would be comparable to posting your bank account number, address, and phone number on a bus station wall.

- Don't follow instructions given by someone you don't know in real life. In fact, never follow someone's instructions unless the implications are fully understood. This will prevent allowing someone to send a destructive program or script to your computer, which could wipe your programs and storage areas clean.

- Don't trust anyone.

IRC is like the Wild West must have been: few controls but not really dangerous unless you find yourself in the path of the wrong desperadoes. Unless you have "eye" contact on IRC—that is, if you try to tangle with the wrong Nethead—you'll not come into conflict with problem users too often. But if you're going to frequent a channel with hard-core, veteran users—for instance, in any channel with the term *warez*, or some variation, in the title, make sure you know what you're doing.

Besides caution, it is also necessary to enter IRC with the ability to turn a blind eye to the exhibitionist, the gender-confused, and the political naifs and waifs ("Capitalism sux, Socialism rools"). The **/list** command, to be discussed shortly, will feed to your screen a report of all IRC channels in use at the moment the command is invoked. The channel names will be given, along with the number of users and the channel *topics*. Topic can be set by users in the channel, so the **list** command can result in a stream of obscenities, perverted pronouncements, and political/anarchic sloganeering—which are actually the channel names and topics—scrolling up your screen. If you can handle it, fine, but be careful of who is in the room with you. It's not difficult to offend the sensitive while on IRC.

Brief Background

Jarkko Oikarinen, of Finland, invented in 1988 what would become IRC, a system for allowing users on his own public BBS to have Internet-style message groups and real-time chats. Oikarinen decided to drop the BBS part of the project altogether and focus on designing a stable, multi-user chat system for the Internet. He used the Bitnet Relay Chat as a model, retaining similar commands and the nickname/channel structure.

Soon afterward, the emerging client/server networking-environment programs were able to handle even more detailed channel and personal information. Oikarinen enlisted friends to help set up a Finnish IRC network with the tolsun.oulu.fi site as the first server.

Eventually, after real-time Internet lines were established between Finland, North America, and other parts of the world, interested networkers at the University of Denver, Oregon State University and elsewhere came online, linking up with the Finland servers.

As of early 1995, the number of IRC servers online at any time wavered at around 100, with between 2,000 and 5,000 users online at any one time.

Using IRC

Beyond the simple warnings given above, IRC can be straightforward but a bit tricky to use. The commands are few (the most commonly used ones, anyway), and they all require a leading slash (/). At times, especially after a long IRC absence or exposure to other command sets, it's difficult to remember this slash. Forgetting to type it, though, will send the command to the channel as text. For instance, typing the line:

```
whois someuser
```

would tell *someuser* (used here as an example, but there's no saying that somewhere sometime someone might not use that as his or her IRC nickname) and everyone else in the channel will know that you were trying to request information on that user. Some might take offense at this. In the least, it will serve to make you a bit more conspicuous and may label you as a newbie (whether you are one or not).

IRC Basics

Following is a basic user guide to IRC. This wide-open medium of chat channels adheres to a system of computing known as *client/server*. This is a division of computing labor that designates more powerful host computers as the servers of satellite, or client, computers, where users sit. These server computers can also be host systems, to which users dial-up or attach their workstations.

The programs running in these servers sometimes differ in the commands available. Most of the commands mentioned below are common to all IRC systems.

Logging On

Normally, to access your host system's IRC *client* software—which will be employed in establishing a connection to an IRC Server—it is necessary simply to type:

```
irc
```

at any command line. This will activate the IRC client if there is one. On systems with a more graphical front-end, there will be a menu choice for IRC, if the system has it available.

When the IRC client logs you on to a server, you'll see a screen like the following (the following log-on occurred January 2, 1995; the screen has been abbreviated.):

```
*** Connecting to port 6667 of server irc-2.mit.edu
*** Welcome to the Internet Relay Network picsirc
*** Your host is irc-2.mit.edu, running version ircd2.8/dog3-
super.p17
*** Your host is irc-2.mit.edu, running version ircd2.8/dog3-
super.p17
*** This server was created Thu Sep 15 1994 at 02: 57:11 EDT
*** There are 2491 users and 1806 invisible on 99 servers
*** There are 84 operators online
*** 4 unknown connection(s)
*** 1414 channels have been formed
*** This server has 308 clients and 7 servers connected
*** - irc-2.mit.edu Message of the Day -
*** - Comments, questions, problems to <irc-admin@MIT.EDU>.
*** -
*** - "Congress shall make no law respecting an establishment
*** - of religion or prohibiting the free exercise thereof;
*** - or abridging the freedom of speech, or of the press; or
*** - the right of the people peaceably to assemble and to
*** - petition the Government for a redress of grievances."
*** - ABSOLUTELY NO BOTS ARE ALLOWED ON THIS SERVER.
*** - The machine irc-2.mit.edu will be rebooted at 2:10 a.m.
*** - be interrupted for a few minutes at these times.
*** -
*** - PLEASE REPORT any new, unusual behavior to mnystrom@mit.edu!
```

Your IRC session has begun.

Netsplit

Occasionally, a server or group of servers will lose their connection to one another, leaving some IRC users separated from the rest of the world. Sometimes, the server you choose will split entirely from the rest of the Internet, and you'll be left only with people logged onto your own server until it rejoins the rest of IRC. This is a *netsplit*. It may take a few minutes to rejoin the Net. Netsplits can be recognized by a sudden logging off of a few or of whole groups of users in your channels. Or you may see an announcement like this:

```
*** Netsplit at 23:20:06 (irc-2.mit.edu exuokmax.ecn.uoknor ).
```

This indicates the time and location of the servers where the break occurred. One remedy for the netsplit is the **/server** command. This, if available, will change your session to a different IRC server, which may still be attached to the larger Web.

Lag

Another source of frequent complaints by Net denizens everywhere, not just on IRC, is *lag*. This Internet is a huge conglomeration of distributed computing power. As such, there may be present at times what can be imagined as online "weather conditions." Your local server can have heavy usage times, in which some of the CPU processing resources are given over to more mundane and businesslike tasks. Local conditions may vary according to loads and usage patterns on nearby computers. Network data packets are trained to route around heavy spots. This, in turn, can lead to other local delay patterns. High usage times over the entire network can cause delays for everyone.

Whatever the cause, a noticeable delay—often of a few seconds, sometimes of more than ten seconds, but occasionally of up to a minute or more—may occur between the time you enter your keystrokes and the time you see the results.

This is *lag*, and it will always be with us, especially since more users are coming in all the time. There are increasingly more bandwidth-hungry graphical applications and some voracious videoconferencing applications tapping the Net, as well.

Lag can sometimes be cured by logging off and on to your host. Sometimes your local session is the problem. Otherwise, the only recourse is to ride it out.

Eventually lags clear, only to reappear again to annoy another time. People spend a lot of lag-producing time cursing it.

IRC Commands

IRC has two basic components: channels and users. Channels have names that begin with the number, or pound, sign (#), such as *#christmas*. Users have names, too. A user's name is known as a *nick* (short for nickname). Nicks can be changed at any time, to anything that is not already being used by someone else. Most commands deal with changing the details of either or both of these components.

Channels, user names, and the commands that manipulate them are not case-sensitive, so there's no need to use capital letters unless, of course, capitals are desired.

So choosing the nick *BilsaBuB* will show up that way to other users, but typing *bilsabub* for commands dealing with the name (by you or others) will work just as well, as will any other combination of upper or lowercase letters.

Each of the next sections will outline a commonly employed IRC command and its usage, in the approximate order in which their uses may be encountered. Be warned that not all clients support all commands. When in doubt, use the **/help** command. (Note: This chapter is not a comprehensive list of all IRC commands, just those most useful to the "average" user. There are many IRC commands for use in scripts and for constructing *bots*. This activity will be discussed briefly at the end of this chapter).

/Help

The **help** command is here, as it is in most online environments. Put a slash in front of it. Once invoked, the help command will feed you whatever local help system is present on your host's client. Help can also be had in the channel *#irchelp*.

/List

Once you get into the IRC system, you will not be automatically sent into any channels. Unless you know where you're going, you *might* want to use the **/list** command to see what's out there—"might" because on typing

/list, the names of *all* the channels currently active in all of IRC will scroll up your screen. Below is a sample result **/list** (obscene titles and topics excised). The real list will be much longer, numbering in the thousands. They'll scroll by fast, so if you're not capturing the text to a file for later browsing, you might just hope that your client supports the **CONTROL-S** key combination (not all do), which will stop the scrolling. **CONTROL-Q** will start it up again. Bail out of the command with **CONTROL-Z**.

```
Channel: Users  Topic

#best:      1
#bergen:    1
#ronsu:     1
#goddess:   1
#insanity: 1
#xfiles:    3
#New_Italy:1
#Nicaragua:1
#angst:     1
#bathtub:   1   Refuge from the world.
Private:    2
Private:    2
#dubuque:   1
#Rive-sud: 1   Yeah!! La rive sud de montreal!
#vampires: 2
#chatzone: 2
#birdhouse:1
#Polskaa:   1
#Cthulhu:   1
```

The list will go on and on, line after line. The first column contains the name of the channel. The second lists the number of users in there at the time. The rest of the line is used for display of a channel topic, if one has been set by a user in the channel. Note also that there are *private* channels listed, and that each channel has a # in front of the name. This symbol is a part of the name, and any channel-related commands must include it.

Minimizing /List

There are a few ways the long list can be limited. Use a wild card (*) to pare the list down. For instance, typing:

```
/list #bb*
```

would result in a list of only those channels that start with the letters "bb." Or typing:

```
/list #a*
```

would result in a list of only those channels starting with the letter "a."

Some parameters that can be used with **/list** include (remember to include each parameter's leading dash):

-MIN n	Where **n** is the minimum number of users on a channel. Those with fewer are not shown.
-MAX n	Where **n** is the maximum number of users on a channel. Those with more are not shown.
-TOPIC	Shows channels that have topics set out for display.

So if you typed:

```
/list -min 5
```

you'd get a list of channels that have at least 5 users in them, such as this:

```
#20plus      9
#inka.de     7
#AmigaGer    8
#KaNAva      8
Prv          7
#lagaule     5
#vaches      5
#russia      5
#Music       6
```

If you typed:

```
/list -topics
```

you'd get a list of only those channels with topics attached, such as this:

```
*** #irchelp   15    Help for IRC. NO bot or script questions
                     will be answered.
*** #cricket   40    D3 Aus5/43 MT11* IH4* MS11 DB3 MW3 MB8
                     StW1 DM2w DG2w AF1w Eng309;T3D1 NZ6/211
*** #iran      10    Watchout for the simple twist of fate...
*** #bsd        4    Berkeley Software Distribution
*** #nin        7    BRYAN8 LOVES FANTASMIC OVER DISNEYLAND
*** #wicca     10    Here There be Bots
*** #taiwan    28    welcome to #Taiwan :)
*** #seoul     29    #seoul is open for chatting once again.
                     Welcome =)
```

```
*** #ubc          4       Univeristy of Brilliant Chinese! :)
*** #unix        26       Just Ask! (man first) No IRC/ DOS/ VMS/
                          Linux/ Cracking Questions
*** #root        31       Congratulations!  You're not running
                          Eunice!
```

These parameters can be used in combination, so that limiting your /list to channels of at least 12 users, say, with topics, would be accomplished by the command:

```
/list -min 12 -topics
```

/Join

After you choose a channel you like *or* if you want to start up an all new channel (with yourself as channel operator), use the **/join** command.

Use this format: **/join #<channel>.** For instance, typing

```
/join #birdhouse
```

will add you to the list of users in that channel. You will then see every public message typed into the channel. If that channel did not exist before you typed the command, it would exist after, and you would be in it.

Join another channel simply by using the command again. You will then be "present" in both channels. The messages in each will be distinguished by the name of the channel at the front of the line.

"Talk"

This is not a command, but once you join a channel, you may want to communicate with those in it. For this, you'd simply type in your message and everyone present would "hear" what you say. Anything typed without a slash in front of it will be interpreted as a public message. Other users will see your lines labeled on the front with the nick of the sender (you) in parentheses, like this:

```
(nick) This message can be seen by all in the channel.
```

The message you type will be echoed back to your screen with a bracket instead of your nick, like this:

```
> This message can be seen by all in the channel.
```

/Msg

This command can be used in this format: **/msg <target> <message>**. It can be used for two purposes:

1. When a user name is the target, **/msg** will send a one-shot private message to that user (continuous private conversations can be accomplished either by making a private channel or by using the **/query** command. See below).

2. When a channel name is the target, the channel will receive a public message from you, whether you are in the channel or not. Private messages will be recognizable because the nick of the sender will be surrounded by asterisks, like this:

```
*nick* I just typed a private message.
```

/Reply

Using **/reply** after receiving such a private message will send a reply to that message's sender.

/Topic

Use this command to set some descriptive topic text out there in the ether for users to see when they run a **/list** command. This is the format: **/topic #<channel> <displayed message>**. For instance:

```
/topic #infinity Join us for endless bandwidth-wasting chatter.
```

will result in a /list looking like this (assuming there are two users in the channel).

```
#infinity     2   Join us for endless bandwidth-wasting chatter.
```

/Mode

The channel operator can change some conditions of the channel. The **/mode** command uses the plus (+) or minus (-) signs to apply or remove a mode from a channel. For instance, typing:

```
/mode #hiding +p
```

would make the channel *#hiding* a private channel like those on the /list screen seen earlier. Typing:

```
/mode #hiding -p
```

would then change it back to public. The plus sign **adds** the mode; the minus sign **takes it away**.

These are some of the more common modes a channel operator can change:

+/- **b**   **Ban**—Use this to ban a user. The format is **/mode #<channelname> +b <nick!emailaddress@dom>** —The user will not be able to join the channel until "unbanned."

+/- **i**   **Invite**—Makes the channel invitation-only.

+/- **k**   **Key**—Makes the channel password-protected. A user cannot join without knowing the key.

+/- **l**   **Limit**—Puts a limit on the number of users who can join the channel.

+/- **n**   **No Outside Messages**—Users from beyond the channel cannot message in.

+/- **o**   **Operator Status**—Gives operator status to another user in the channel.

+/- **p**   **Private**—Makes the channel private.

+/- **s**   **Secret**—Makes the channel "secret" (it doesn't show up on the /list screen at all).

+/- **t**   **Topic**—Makes the channel's topic changeable by the channel operator only.

/Invite

When a channel is in "invite mode," use the command **/invite <nick>** to call someone into the channel.

/Ignore

If a user is persistently annoying, use **/ignore <nick>** to prevent all messages generated by that user from reaching your screen.

/Away

The **/away** command allows you to attach a message to your nick while it's still active in the IRC system. If you are away from your computer and you're expecting someone, she will see this message if she checks your nick with the **/whois** command. Use the format **/away <message>**.

/Whois

Used in this format, **/whois <nick>** gives the e-mail address, originating host information and the channels currently occupied by that nick.

/Whowas

This does the same as **/whois** for a user who recently left the system.

/Names

This command will scroll out the nicks on a particular public channel. Use this format: **/names #<channelname>**. Be careful to type *something* after the command here, so that you'll get either the names in the target channel or an error message. Leaving a blank space will result in the procession of *all* the names in public channels across your screen.

/Query

If you intend to have a long-running private conversation, you can use **/query**. This command, followed by one or more nicks (separated by commas, no space) will initiate a continuous private conversation. The connection stays active until the command alone, **/query,** with no names after it, is typed again. All messages following activation will be passed to the target user(s).

/Kick

If you are a channel operator and want someone out of the channel, use the command **/KICK <nick> <message>**. Add a message after the nick to supply a farewell or reason to the kicked user, or to add insult to injury.

/Dcc

This stands for *direct client connection*. File transfers and direct-link chats are possible with the **/dcc** command. Check for details on usage in the help files of your local server.

/Part

With this command, you can leave any individual channel. Use the format **/part #<channelname>**. It's the exiting counterpart to **/join #<channelname>**.

/Quit

Use **/quit** to leave IRC.

Happy Channeling

Look at the information that comes with the **/help** command if you feel the need for more detail—for instance, if you want to program scripts or bots. Otherwise, go to it. And be careful out there.

Scripts and Bots

A simple script is a preconstructed message or series of messages that you can design to perform tasks ranging from drawing a simple picture in an IRC channel to flooding a nick with an attack of text.

An elaborate, self-sustaining, decision-making script can be called a *bot*. It's an automatic process that an advanced user can attach to an IRC channel to read and react to messages typed into the channel, or messages sent directly to it with the **/msg** command. A *warbot* is designed for use against other users or against IRC itself. Bots meant to do harm are one reason why many servers have banned their presence. Other servers allow them, though, and some with bans might make exceptions for trusted users with useful bots.

Dan Brown runs a script bot that moderates a simulation of a science fiction adventure on a channel called *#starfleet*. According to Brown, making a simple bot doesn't require an extensive knowledge of programming and can provide valuable programming experience.

"I never had much experience in computer programming before running IRC robots, besides some BASIC programming," Brown says. "IRC II [a UNIX-based IRC client] is the most-used client all over IRC. Its programming language has been modeled after C [a popular programming language], so anyone who has had C programming experience will be somewhat familiar with IRC II programming. The simplest IRC robot will simply join a channel and respond to what people say to it. JoeBot—a name I'll use and [which] has no relation to any robots that may or may not be on IRC—would just join the channel *#chat*, and respond to someone saying 'hi joebot.' And that's just a minimum. The maximum, however, is almost limitless.... There's a limit to how much any language can express ideas, but the amount of intelligence that IRC robots achieve is always shoved up to the next marker every time a bot programmer thinks of something ingenious."

Belly Up

If, sometime while in IRC, you typed:

```
/join #ircbar
```

you would probably be greeted by a bot that "tends bar" in the gathering place that exists in that channel.

As in the sample below, the first line seen after joining a channel is a message from the system reporting the "change":

```
*** Change: bilsabub has joined channel #ircbar
```

```
*** Topic on channel #ircbar is ANNOUNCEMENT - If you have any
trouble contact Joshua_WG or RedRum

*** Users on #ircbar: bilsabub Myrlyn @Barman4 NoSioP kevin-
helpcafe Delsion Skyer RRDetachd
```

When you join, the occupants of the channel will be listed. The topic
in the channel is controlled by the bot that acts as host, which also greets
all newcomers:

```
-Barman4- Welcome to the #IRCBar bilsabub. I am your bot Barman!
-Barman4- ==== If you have any trouble use /msg barman4 help
====
(Myrlyn) Hi bil
> Heya
*** Change: SPIKER (esimoni@mason1.gmu.edu) has joined channel
#ircbar
(Myrlyn) Hi spike
(SPIKER) Hi
```

The barman bot changes the topic periodically. Ask for the barman's
help files with this command:

```
/msg barman4 help
H-Barman4- Hi I am Barman4. I am a BOT for the #IRCBar
H-Barman4- channel. My main job is to serve drinks to all
H-Barman4- the customers.  But I also have a limited
H-Barman4- amount of other functions.
```

People tend to come and go.

```
*** Change: SPIKER has left Channel
*** Topic on channel #ircbar changed to Get your butt in here,
have a drink, have lots more drinks, then passout!
<Skyer> bilsabub
<milamber> I've never read any lovecraft. I have seen some
movies though

> lovecraft movies?
<milamber> Yeah, like From Beyond. I forgot the name of the
other one I saw
> hm. Wouldn't Mountains of ma...ahem, scuse me...mountains of
madness make a good movie?

<Delsion>   \'X.X'
<Delsion>   =(___)=
<Delsion>      U
<Delsion>   MEOW!!!
```

This last bit is an example of a short script, ostensibly a picture of a cat:

```
** Barman4 has changed the topic on channel #ircbar to Don't come
in unless you like Fun, Frolics and alcohol abuse!
```

Order a drink from the barman by typing one of a group of natural-sounding messages right into the channel:

```
> barman can i have a dinkelacker_ocktoberfest (beer)
```

Whatever your order is will result in:

```
-Barman4:#ircbar- ==== Gets bilsabub a dinkelacker_ocktoberfest
(beer)
<milamber> I'm outta here, have a happy new year all =)
<Delsion> hoi kiria
-Barman4:#ircbar- ==== It's nice to see people happy! ====
```

The bot in *#ircbar* was programmed by Andrew Cardwell. He recounts the history in the following electronic newsletter:

The History Of Barman

Barman originally appeared on IRC some three years ago. The idea was born just after a Christmas holiday, when I learnt about IRC and the fact people could run bots on it. So I set off working my way through the BotDoc, looking at example code [and] trying to develop my idea into a somewhat sensible bot, namely Barman.

Eventually I finished my creation, although a little crude. I was proud of the bot. The first trouble I had was getting Barman to stay on. It seemed that there was already a Barman floating around the world of IRC, and he was colliding the bot because it was using his nick. So was born Barman1.

The channel I and the bot began on was *#europe*, a little-known channel mainly populated by the French and a few of us British. Next we went to a channel called *#Eurobar*, but here we had problems as I developed Barman2. A year later I started *#IRCBar*, now home and final resting place of the famous barbot.

Barman3 came shortly after and was a major rewrite. Many of Barman's help and other functions appeared in this version. But the bot was becoming slow, so along came Barman4—still a script bot but using superior scripts. Barman4 was a joint effort between myself (Joshua_WG) and RedRum. Amongst other improved features we [modularized] the bot so his features could be used and edited with ease.

(continues)

Barguard appeared not long after. He was just the most simple bot you can imagine, using one of Barman4's modules to op [grant operator privileges to] the relevant people and op Barman in case he should somehow lose ops.

That brings us right up to date, except at the moment I am currently working on BarDog and Barman5. These new bots will replace Barman4 and Barguard and should hopefully appear sometime in the new year.

Joshua_WG

Deal

Or, on the other hand, you may stumble on something like this:

```
(PBot) vinal, you're next.
(Gridlock) well, enough bad luck for me
(PBot) vinal checks.
(PBot) Scorpion, you're next.
(Gridlock) ;)
(PBot) Gridlock folds and mumbles, "Again!"  2 players remain-
ing.
(PBot) Scorpion has set the bet to 20. Pot is 158.
(PBot) vinal, you're next.
(PBot) vinal folds and mumbles, "not".  1 players remaining.
(PBot) Scorpion wins the game with 158 in the pot.
(Scorpion) still not a fool ehh??
(PBot) Game #9015 is starting.  Everyone pay ante of 10.
```

It's a poker game, run and dealt by a bot named Pbot.

This tableau unfolds in a channel called *#poker* (there's also a *#poker2*). Spectators are welcome. To join in the game, obtain an account. Type:

```
/msg pbot help
```

while in the channel to find out how.

The *#poker* channel's present keeper is Pierre "Lyverbe" Fournier. He has modified a bot originated by Rudy "Radix" Amid. The following account of its invention is from the PBot help files (reproduced with permission):

Originally, the idea came to me in early 1993. After the success of my first IRC bot game, MooBot, I went on to think that someone will be inspired to make a poker bot. Of course, no one seemed to have the time nor the inclination to make such a bot, so I went on in February 1993 to start making a poker bot.

I completed an alpha version of PokerBot in late February and tested it on IRC. It wasn't as easy as I expected; the bot was riddled with all sorts of mysterious bugs as I was testing the user interface aspect of it. The bot was written with IRC II scripts, and the poker module was written in C.

It didn't take long for me to realize this: [an] 80 percent IRC II-scripts bot was not fast and powerful—but it was the best way to debug and perfect the command line parsing [reading and interpreting commands from the channel], recompiling the program on the fly without killing the bot. By March 1993, I started to put the poker module together as one big C program, eliminating the need to rely on IRC II scripts to parse the commands. The bot at this point had many commands and was flexible enough to program. From then on, I concentrated on the poker game itself.

By late March, I was ready for PBot's beta-testing. I called on a few dedicated users on IRC to discuss ideas and play the game. There were lots of ideas and modifications to be made. Tweaking the program proved to be the hardest. Slowly, after one feature was added at a time, bugs appeared and were subsequently debugged. The process was painstakingly slow, but I was determined to get it up and running, as I [knew] this bot [would] prove to be the best bot that ever happened to IRC. After my exams in April, I started to work full-time on this bot, spending countless hours modifying and testing with my beta-testers. Ideas kept pouring in.

Finally, in June, I had a fully functional poker bot! Modifications did not stop then, but it was time for me to slow down and let the bot make itself known to the world. In August, I had to leave the country for a few months and [gave] this bot to Lyverbe for safekeeping, continued maintenance, and development of PBot.

PBot is one of my best programming projects. I had fun, cried, died, laughed, and learned a lot during its development. Moreover, I made a lot of friends, which is always nice. >

Here's a sample of a complete hand as it occurred in the *#poker* channel:

```
(PBot) Game #9021 is starting.  Everyone pay ante of 10._
(PBot) $: ***:0      Sco:195     bil:137    Beh:18583  bei:230
Sly:2734
```

The bot reports the players at the start of a hand—the names are abbreviated to three letters—and the size of their wads (measured in units of unidentified currency. IRCbucks?) Seat one in this example is empty.

```
PBot- Your cards: 1) 7-S   2) 10-C   3) 5-H   4) 6-S   5) 2-C
```

The bot deals your hand. Cards are numbered 1 to 5. Suits are represented by letters. S is spades, C is clubs, H is hearts, D is diamonds. This hand isn't showing much.

```
(PBot) being_, you're first to place a bet.
```

Responses to the bot can be made with a **/msg pbot <command>** or by typing **p <command>** in the open channel.

```
(PBot) being_ checks.
```

being_ probably typed **/msg pbot bet 0** to accomplish the pass.

```
(PBot) Sly, you're next.
(Sly) p bet
```

Sly responds with a public message, betting nothing.

```
(PBot) Sly checks.
(PBot) Scorpion, you're next.
(PBot) Scorpion checks.
(PBot) bilsabub, you're next.
-PBot- It is your turn: make a bet.
```

Typing in the command:

```
/msg PBot bet 0
```

will communicate the bet to the bot.

```
(PBot) bilsabub checks.
(PBot) Behemoth, you're next.
(PBot) Behemoth checks._[23;1H
(PBot) Everyone has bet.  Now indicate which cards to discard.
(Sly) p discard 2 4 5
```

Drop cards using their numbers, either publicly or with a **/msg** command.

```
(PBot) Behemoth will be discarding 2 cards.
(PBot) Scorpion will be discarding 2 cards.
(Sly) p discard 2 4 5
(PBot) being_ will be discarding 1 card._
(PBot) Sly will be discarding 3 cards.
-PBot- It is your turn: discard cards. (7-S 10-C  5-H  6-S  2-C)

> p discard 2 5

(PBot) bilsabub will be discarding 2 cards.
```

The bot deals two more cards:

```
-PBot- Your cards: 1) 7-S   2) A-C   3) 5-H   4) 6-S   5) 6-C
```

A pair of sixes, enough to stay in this hand, unless the price goes way up.

```
(PBot) Discarded cards replaced.  It's time to place final bets!
(PBot) being_, you're first to place a bet.
(PBot) being_ checks.
(PBot) Sly, you're next.
(Sly) p bet 1
(PBot) Sly has set the bet to 1. Pot is 51.
(PBot) Scorpion, you're next.
(PBot) Scorpion folds.  4 players remaining.
(PBot) bilsabub, you're next.
-PBot- It is your turn: make a bet or call cards.
(PBot) being_ folds.  3 players remaining.
```

Hang in there. Not much action in this hand.

```
> p bet 1

(PBot) bilsabub pays 1 to see the bet. Pot is 52.
(PBot) Behemoth, you're next.
(PBot) Behemoth pays 1 to see the bet. Pot is 53.
(PBot) Revealing the players' cards:
(PBot)  bilsabub: 7-S  A-C  5-H  6-S  6-C  Behemoth: 4-H  3-D  K-
S  3-S  J-S  Sly:10-S  A-S 10-D  2-S  8-D
(PBot) Sly's hand value: A pair of 10s.
(PBot) Sly wins the game with 53 in the pot.
```

A pair of tens beats a pair of sixes, Oh well.

IRC, the Wild West of the Electronic Frontier

For its lack of controls, the IRC "cloud" has gained a seedy reputation, much of it deserved. But with proper precautions—and the expectation that eventually you *will* be /**kicked**, insulted, or otherwise abused and offended—it's possible to explore this popular mass-chatting environment mostly unscathed.

IRC Common Commands Summary	
/**ignore**	Kills off messages from a user before they reach you.
/**invite** \<user\> \<channel\>	Invites a user into a channel (channel operator).
/**join** #\<channel\>	Allows you to enter a channel.
/**kick** \<channel\> \<nickname\> \<comment\>	Forces a user off a channel. Comments attached to the announcement of the change may be the reason the person is getting /kicked.
/**list**	Lists all channels; limiters include -min, -max, -topic.
/**mode** \<channel\> +/- o,p,s,i,t,n,l,b,k	Operator Modes o—Gives channel operator privileges to another. p—Makes a channel private. s—Makes a channel secret. i—Makes a channel invitation-only. t—Sets topic (channel operator). n—"No messages to channel" from outside. l—Limits the number of users in the channel. b—Bans a user from the channel. k—Sets a password.

continues

IRC Common Commands Summary (continued)

Command	Description
/msg <nickname>|<channel> <message>	Sends a private message to a user or public message to a channel.
/names <channel>	Lists all nicks in the channel.
/nick <nickname>	Originates or changes a nickname.
/part #<channelname>	Allows you to leave a channel.
/query	Establishes an extended private conversation.
/quit	Signs you off.
/reply	Answers the user who last sent you a /msg.
/topic <channel> <message>	Sets or changes the topic of the channel.
/whois <nick>	Provides information on someone in the channel.
/whowas <nick>	Provides information on someone who recently left the channel.

Chapter 7

Doing It Yourself

ven without the resources of a large institution to help you pursue your interactive Internetting interests, an individual or small organization can still achieve a certain capability without too much cost. And it's not necessary to be an expert in that family of venerable computer operating systems that refuses to die—UNIX.

Detailed technical procedures about UNIX clients and servers would be beyond the scope of this book. Refer to the Appendix for a portion of Jennifer Smith's MUD FAQ (available for file transfer at **ftp.math.okstate.edu** in the directory **pub/muds/misc/mud-faq**). Part 2 of the FAQ contains the latest comprehensive information on MUD clients, servers, and what it takes to run them. This is the section of the FAQ that changes the most, according to Smith. Outlined there are the server types, the systems on which they will run, and the client programs that can be used for access.

For those interested in gaining familiarity with UNIX of some type, there is a freeware version of a UNIX-like operating system called LINUX.

LINUX, as freeware, has a large following, with Usenet newsgroups devoted to its discussion. It's regarded, in some quarters, as a strong competitor for the commercial "brands" of UNIX (an operating system invented a quarter century ago). And the price is right, free (a CD-ROM with LINUX is available for $39.95 from Walnut Creek CDROM, 800-786-9907, voice).

LINUX supports all the front-line networking needed to create interactive environments, so if running a networked MUD holds some interest and funds are limited, look into LINUX.

A Server

What we can do here is provide a taste of what can be had for an MS-DOS-based system. There is a server called *LPmud for DOS*. It requires a 386 compatible system or better to run. There is no network support at this point, but it can be run from console sessions (the keyboard) or through serial port connections (and so through modems, like a regular BBS). So, the LPmud for DOS could be used for adventuring by a few friends over the phone or modified for use by a small organization or business in need of an interactive environment on the cheap. The *LPmud for DOS* is a port of the popular LPmud designed by Lars Pensjl. The DOS version was conjured up by Werner Almesberger, with further refinements by Olav Kolbu.

Get the Archive

Retrieve the archive file that contains *LPmud for DOS* from a site listed in the FAQ, such as **ftp.lysator.liu.se**.

Then travel to the directory:

```
/pub/lpmud
```

Do a **ls -l** (list long form), and you'll see two files:

```
ok312exe.exe
ok312lib.exe
```

The first, ok312exe.exe, contains only the executable files needed to run the LPmud for DOS server. It does not include a *mudlib*.

Mudlib is a shortened form of the term MUD library. A *mudlib* is the database of rooms and objects that the mud administrator builds into the environment. The first file, **ok312exe.exe** would be of use to someone who already has access to a *mudlib*. It has the server's executable files only.

Someone without a mudlib in hand would want to retrieve both these archives. **Ok312lib.exe** contains a mudlib set of room and object files that is ready to roll.

Open the Files

Once retrieved to your own computer (after doing whatever needs to be done through FTP, then transferring or downloading to your system), make a directory called:

```
1pmud
```

This will be the only directory you'll need to create. Then move the archive file or files into that directory and **run** them. The files will extract themselves and create the complex directory structure that organizes the MUD.

Read the Docs

For more information on the serial port connections or connecting some modems, refer to the **readme.1st** file in the **\lpmud\docs** directory. Refer to this file and the documentation that comes with your modem(s) to coordinate the *comdrv* (the *communications driver* settings needed to run connections to the MUD through your serial ports).

Also, explore the directory structure you just created. There are many subdirectories under the **\lib245** directory that contain information on building (building in general will be covered in a later section, with a different MUD system).

Configure the System

This MUD, like many, is highly demanding of system resources, so most of the device drivers and *TSRs* (*Terminate and Stay Resident*) programs that linger in RAM will have to be removed. Create a system, or boot disk, with **autoexec.bat** and **config.sys** files like the ones below. If you have DOS 6.x, you can accomplished the same by adding such a configuration as a choice if you've made use of the multiple configuration capabilities of that version.

```
Autoexec.bat for LPmud for DOS
prompt $P$G
PATH c:\;C:\DOS;C:\LPMUD\BIN
SET GO32TMP=C:/TMP
SET GO32=ansi driver C:/LPMUD/drivers/paradise.grd gw 1024 gh 768
tw 132 th 43 emu
C:/lpmud/bin/emu387
SET SERIAL=C:/lpmud/lines
SET HOME=C:/lpmud/bin
Config.sys file LPmud for DOS

shell=command.com /e:512 /p
install=c:\dos\share.exe
device=c:\dos\ansi.sys
device=c:\dmdrvr.bin
buffers=30
files=40
```

The settings for both these files can be lifted electronically from the **autoxbat.smp** and **cfgsys.smp** files to be found in the **\lpmud\docs** directory for pasting into the files on your system.

Reboot or reload your new configuration. You'll notice that the PATH statement in the **autoexec.bat** file listed above includes the **\lpmud\bin** directory. This means any files in that directory can be run from any other directory on your system. Start the MUD with the command:

```
pars312c
```

This initializes the MUD parser, the program that reads and interprets player commands. The screen will blank and a message will appear at the bottom:

```
#1 [AVAILABLE].
```

This means that the MUD is running, and the first channel is open. Hit ENTER, and the message will change to:

```
#1 CONNECTED
```

You have just established a session on your own MUD. Press ENTER and the "welcome screen" will appear:

```
Welcome to <Fill in a good name here> (LPmud 2.4.5)
Administrator and supreme ruler: <Your name here>
username:
Version: 03.01.02
What is your name:
```

Type in the preset wizard account:

```
aragorn
```

No password is necessary, but if you will be opening the system up to others, you will want to set one. Type "**help**" for a list of commands. Type "**help wizard**" for a list of wizard commands. Use ALT-S to drop out to a DOS shell for editing files of files. Good luck. From here you're on your own.

And if you go in as a player, don't worry the first time you die. An LPmud for DOS incarnation of a certain "Lars" will appear and make a case for you with the Grim Reaper. He has a lot of pull in these parts.

A MUD Client

The choice of client will differ depending on the MUD you're calling. If you don't have a direct connection to the Net yourself, the system you call, or access by workstation, will have to have one installed. In matters like this, and in all matters of system resource usage, you'll have to get the system administration's aid and permission to install one. Again, refer to Smith's FAQ in the Appendix for information on, and the locations of, clients.

There is one program, however, which can run under Microsoft Windows and can be used for all MUDs. It's a simple, graphical, universal MUD front-end called MUDman.

At the time of this writing, one place this program could be had for FTP was at **ftp.jussieu.fr** in the **/pub3/pc/win3/misc** directory. The file is named **mudman12.zip**. This zip archive will require the shareware file compression software PKZip to unpack it. Most FTP sites have a version of this popular program available.

To use MUDman, just install it as you would any new Windows program and click on the icon. The program will run and direct you to use whatever communication method is usually employed for accessing a MUD.

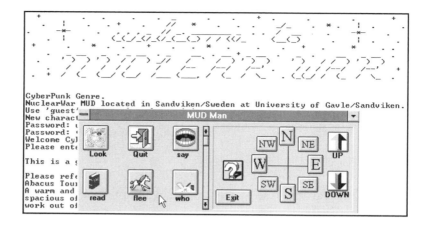

Once there, you will see a control panel inset appear over your screen, as below:

The MUDman client provides a directional compass for easy navigation around any MUD in which the standard directions can move your character about. There are nine buttons to be programmed with the actions or dialogue used most often. On each macro's button, a colorful icon can be pasted. MUDman is shareware, with an extremely reasonable price of $9. The registered version entitles the user to more buttons and pictures.

> **Tip:** One disadvantage of MUDman is that it cannot be used for multiple MUDs, unless you want to use the same customized commands everywhere. To use it at multiple MUDs with commands that vary, just copy the contents of the entire directory into some other uniquely named directory and run another version for however many MUDs you call.

MUD Object-Oriented

Client/server, the meshing of the two concepts just covered, is a widely-used buzzword for a trend in computing in which the processing power of any large, Internetted system is distributed somewhat evenly over the system. In contrast, in the older model, all the computer mule flesh was held in a central glass house, attended by priestly expert acolytes. Client/ server is sometimes elusive to achieve successfully, but it's an ever more desirable computing model for which many organizations now strive. The practice of using the home or office computer's processing power to access local BBSs or more powerful Internetted server systems constitutes a form of client/server.

Another trendy buzz phrase encountered among the experts (and in their literature) is known as *object-oriented programming*. This is another elusive ideal to achieve, and a concept equally elusive to define. Simplistically, object-oriented describes a more modularized system of programming a computer, which allows processes and functions to exhibit similar behaviors under many differing conditions or inputs. In other words, a package of data (an object) can be fitted with characteristics that may be accessible no matter what type of (object compatible) process or software is used to manipulate it.

You can experience object-oriented in action—in fact, you can immerse yourself in it—in any of the numerous MOO (MUD, Object-Oriented) systems on the Internet.

MOO was developed by Pavel Curtis and the Xerox Palo Alto Research Center, the fabled Xerox PARC where most of the concepts defining modern microcomputers were invented (such as laser printers, GUI, the mouse). The home field MOO at PARC is **LambdaMOO (lambda.parc.xerox.com 8888)**.

Systems running the MOO environment are extensible, which means that the players cannot program the actual parser or interpreter. Still, players can effect elaborate and complex improvements or extensions through the use of an easily understood programming language.

Most MUDs have some limited extensibility, most often held up as an ultimate goal for which to strive for wizard status. Conversely, most MOO systems allow all members in good standing to create and alter the environment.

At **LambdaMOO**, you can get an account with the command:

```
@request a character
```

You'll have to provide your correct e-mail address and answer some questions. Lambda is a popular destination and at times can have 200 or more accounts accessing it at the same time. This makes for some mighty lag. It also makes for a fitting crucible, since Lambda is not only an illustration of object-based user programmability, but also an experiment in online democracy.

More peaceful and less laggy is the MediaMOO system, physically located at the Massachusetts Institute of Technology's renowned Media Lab. Membership is restricted to media researchers, students, and other interested parties, but guest accounts are available for visits by anyone. Just type:

```
@connect guest
```

and you're in.

The examples in this section were made there (and, I hope, can still be seen there if you happen by).

MOOgramming

Before venturing to program a MOO object, a thorough reading of the MOO programmer manual would be wise. It and other interesting documents—such as electronic versions of many academic papers available on MUDding and MOO programming tutorials—are available for FTP at **ftp.parc.xerox.com** in the **pub/MOO/contrib/docs** directory.

Once you have a character on a MOO system (guests can't alter the MOO), you will have an online avatar through which to act and interact with others from all over the world. Customize your environment with some of the following procedures. The examples given are simple, using only the most basic commands. Like most programming languages, there are deeper levels of complexity. Once you master them, you'll be able to create more complicated objects that react to stimuli in surprising and intriguing ways.

Living Space

Build additions to the MOO topography with the **@dig** command. Use this format:

```
@dig <new room name>
```

This will create a new room with the name given after the command. For example, my own character, "Bones" (an old nickname), needed a place to live. To start construction of a home, I used this command:

```
@dig The BonesYard
```

This created a container object called "The BonesYard."

Make exits for the room with the following variations of **@dig**:

```
@dig <exit text> to <new-room-name>
@dig <exit text> to <old-room-object-number>
```

where <exit text> is any term that will serve as the command to exit that room. You can only make exits from rooms you own, though, so in order to get an "entrance" to your room from somewhere else, ask another player to make one. For example, this command makes an exit from The BonesYard to MediaMoo's Library:

```
@dig up to The Library
```

This means that when a player enters The BonesYard, or, once in there, gives the **look** command, the description will appear, along with:

```
Obvious exits: Up to The Library.
```

Sethome

The BonesYard became home for the Bones character with the **@sethome** command. It will make whatever room the character occupies at that moment the home for that character. Home is the place your character will appear at the start of all logons thereafter, unless changed.

Describe

In the MOO systems, you'll find room objects, player objects, and thing or container objects—among others. The object classes exhibit some differences, but many classes have certain properties in common. All objects have numbers, for instance, which can be used in commands in place of the sometimes lengthy text names. All objects can also be embellished with text descriptions. The format is:

```
@describe <object (or object #)> as <descriptive text>
```

For instance, the BonesYard got its description with:

```
@describe The BonesYard as A veritable charnel house of books.
Every vertical surface is covered by the dusty volumes, even the
back of the door. From a hook on a shelf hangs a framed image of,
what else? Books. On the image is a quotation, Books: the bones
of minds long gone.
```

Anytime a character enters that room, or types a **look** command while in the room, she will see this description:

```
A veritable charnel house of books. Every vertical surface is
covered by the dusty volumes, even the back of the door. From a
hook on a shelf hangs a framed image of, what else? Books. On the
image is a quotation, Books: the bones of minds long gone.
```

Recycle

If, at any time, you are not happy with an object, use the **@recycle** command to delete it:

```
@recycle <object>
```

> **Tip:** Your home may be a place of initial logon or it may be the headquarters for your important MOOgramming sessions. Since it is something you own (all objects are owned by someone, or some thing), you can set all its properties or, with more **moo**gramming skill, make up new ones. Even though properties are too involving of a topic for this short volume, there's one that you can use on the fly in case you want some privacy in your home. It's the free_entry property. Use the following
>
> (continues)

(continued)
command to alter this property for the home room you own. The leading semicolon tells the MOO to interpret the line as if it were a program:

```
;player.home.free_entry = 0
```

This closes the room to outsiders. To reverse it, type:

```
;player.home.free_entry = 1
```

Looking Around

Next, you might want to conjure up an object to put in your room. In a MOO, you can either walk from room to room or teleport around to places you know.

@join can be used to travel to the location of a character. Use it, perhaps, to join someone after a **@who** query, which gives a list of players online at the moment.

Use **@go** to teleport to a named room. Here's an example:

```
@go Memorial Drive
```

When you arrive, you'll see this description:

```
Memorial Drive
A wide boulevard with a park-like center strip, where you are
standing at the moment. Cars are zipping by at dangerous speeds.
To the north is Building E51 on the MIT Campus. To the south is
the STS Centre, an ultra-modern building cantilevered over the
Charles River.
Obvious exits: north to E51 First Floor Lobby, south to STS
Centre Lounge, and northwest to Recyclable #855.
You see Maple Tree here.
```

After a few moments, a message appears on the screen:

```
Avoid nasty chemicals.
```

But as far as you can tell, you're the only one here. Then another message appears:

```
Don't spray me!
```

And another:

```
Stop clearcutting!
```

And another:

```
Climb me.
```

Soon you begin to suspect that it's the

```
Maple Syrup
```

tree that's doing the talking.

```
Are you listening to me?
```

There's a talking tree at MediaMOO:

```
There is no immortality, but a tree's love!
```

Now wouldn't something like that be an interesting object for a certain BonesYard? Though another talking tree would be derivative, to say the least, there are definitely some possibilities.

Use the **@examine** command to take a closer look at the properties of the tree:

```
@examine Maple Tree
```

The result is an accounting of many secrets in the wood of this tree:

```
Maple Tree (#1598) is owned by Wade (#535).
An ordinary-looking maple tree that's treated with special
chemicals developed by MIT biologists to keep it green and leafy
year-round.
Obvious Verbs:
  climb tree
  list tree
  record <anything> on tree
  erase <anything> on tree
  @wait_time/@react_time/@identified tree is <anything>
  @lockmsg tree with <anything>
  @unlockmsg tree
  teach tree for <anything>
  poke tree
  show_erased tree
  remove_erased tree
  g*et/t*ake tree
  d/th*row tree
  gi*ve/ha*nd tree to <anything>
```

First is the name of the tree and its owner (plus their numbers). Next is the object's description, followed by a list of "Obvious Verbs." A verb is an extremely important MOO programming feature. As in spoken language, a verb makes things happen. Editing verbs is nearly synonymous with the term programming on a MOO. We'll see some simple verb editing in a bit.

You'll notice that there's a verb for recording messages "on" the tree. To try it, type:

```
record Hug children. They don't give splinters. on tree
```

Before you know it, the tree recites:

```
Hug children. They don't give splinters.
```

We'd like to make a copy of this object. To do this, we'll have to see what the object's parent is. The MOO system is a set of "family" relationships between objects and their children. When you make a child of an object, that child inherits all the properties of that object.

Use the **@parent** command to get the object family tree of this tree, like so:

```
@parent maple tree
```

Or you could substitute the object's number, now that it's known:

```
@parent #1598
```

Here's the result:

```
Maple Tree(#1598)    Generic Announcer(#1019)    generic thing(#5)
Root Class(#1)
```

The tree's inheritance began, as all MOO things do, as a "Root Class" object. From that was created a "generic thing." Someone with a bit of MOOgramming wizardry then made a "Generic Announcer," an object on which words can be recorded, and from which they can be repeated.

It's simple, then, to take a copy of that object and rename it for yourself. Use the very god-like and satisfying **@create** command, in this format:

```
@create <name or number of object being copied> called <new
object name>
```

For example:

```
@create #1019 called Quoteinator
```

The system reports:

```
You now have Quoteinator with object number #6808 and parent
Generic Announcer (#1019).
```

Add a description (and since the name is a bit hard to type, use the object number):

```
@describe #6808 as A small box in a cloth sack, similar to one of
those novelties that laugh, 'Haw haw haw haw....' Except this one
doesn't laugh. It just spouts quotes endlessly. And worse—the
quotes are all about writing.
```

Now, to record a bunch of quotes, just like with the tree:

```
record Success and failure are equally disastrous. - Tennessee
Williams on quoteinator
```

The Quoteinator, when full, will quote writers:

```
Success and failure are equally disastrous. - Tennessee Williams

If I could think, maybe I wouldn't write. - Scott Spencer

Ignorance is one of the sources of poetry. - Wallace Stevens

You lose it if you talk about it. - Ernest Hemingway

A best-seller is the guilded tomb of a mediocre talent. - L.P.
Smith
```

Verbs

We head back home to the BonesYard, with Quoteinator securely and quietly in tow (it's mute when held). The room could sure use at least one piece of furniture. If you don't want an object that will inherit a lot of properties, you can get real basic and start from (near) scratch:

```
@ create #5 called the nicest piano in existence
```

This copies "generic thing" (#5) to an object called "the nicest piano in existence."

Describe it:

```
@describe the nicest piano in the world as A stunning ebony
Steinway.
```

One of the many tips given by MediaMOO administrators is that when creating an object, one should assume that people will try to manipulate it. You might want to anticipate what people who come across your object are likely to try to do with it. If a guest in the BonesYard should feel like using the piano, she shouldn't be completely disappointed if she tries. This is where the verbs come in.

Before we discuss verbs and their editing, however, it might be useful to put yourself in the shoes of someone who wants to use the piano. She might not think to type out its whole name as it was given by its creator:

```
play the nicest piano in the world
```

But she might type:

```
play piano
```

To anticipate this eventuality, you can assign an alias, or substitute word, for the object. All aliases are treated the same way as the real name, and the object number. Here's the format for assigning an alias:

```
@addalias <alias> to <object>
```

So to assign the word *piano* to the object, you would write

```
@addalias piano to #8636
```

This prepares for the time when the verb play is associated with object #8636, AKA piano.

Editing Verbs

Wade Roush, a science writer, is the Wade character who created the tree that stands blabbering on Memorial Drive, a fine creation. We can study his technique further by looking at his other objects. To look at all the objects owned by a player, and to scout out techniques for programming objects of your own, use the command:

```
@audit wade
```

Here's a list representing a tiny portion of Wade's many objects:

```
 3K  #1148 Generic Statue          [Cardboard Box]
 1K  #1149 Statue of Bruno Latour  [STS Centre Balcony]
12K  #1150 The Quotation Machine   [STS Centre 3rd Level Hall]
 4K  #1591 How to Get to Other MUDs [STS Bulletin Board]
 1K  #1594 Grandfather Clock       [STS Centre Lounge]
 3K  #1598 Maple Tree              [Memorial Drive]
```

This list gives the system memory space taken up by the object (in kilobytes), its number, name and current location. There's that talkative tree, and it looks like there's a similar machine for generating quotes already present in the MOO. You can be sure it's more elaborate than our little Quoteinator. To take a look, type:

```
@examine #1150
```

You'll get a list of facts and verbs on this object:

```
The Quotation Machine (#1150) is owned by Wade (#535).
Aliases:  The Quotation Machine, quotation machine, quotation,
and machine
An odd-looking black box, about a meter high, with Bose speakers
attached to the sides. There is a lever on top that moves forward
and backward in a slot. The near end of the slot is labeled "Gems
of Wisdom," and the far end is labeled "Hot Air." To learn how to
use the machine, type:  help machine
Obvious Verbs:
  push <anything> on #1150
  pull <anything> on #1150
  addair #1150 is <anything>
  addgem #1150 is <anything>
  g*et/t*ake #1150
  d*rop/th*row #1150
  gi*ve/ha*nd #1150 to <anything>
```

Significant here are the top two verbs, push and pull. These actions might be programmed similar enough to our intended action for the piano object—play. Seeing the way they're handled might help make our task a little easier.

To look at the programming in an object, use the **@dump** command. We won't show the coding of all the action in the object, but here's the part on the pull verb that helps us (each line ends with a semicolon):

```
player:tell(((("You " + verb) + " the lever on ") + this.name) +
".");
this.location:announce((((((player.name + " ") + verb) + "s the
lever on") + this.name) + ".");
```

We want some programming that announces something to the person who activates it, as well as to others in the room, since playing a piano will affect everyone present. The above snippet of Wade's code does that. Translated, the first line above says:

```
To the player activating this verb, tell "Activating player's
name pulls the lever on The Quotation Machine."
```

That's the announcement to the activating player. The term *this name* refers to is the machine's name. This is a term reserved for the activated object.

The second line translates as:

```
Make the room where this action occurs announce, "The activating
player pulls the lever on The Quotation Machine."
```

We can use this.

To make the piano "playable," use the command to create the verb:

```
@verb piano:play this
```

All verbs have the capability of relating to a direct object, a preposition, and an indirect object, if desired or suitable for the grammatical sense of the verb's usage. See the programmer's documentation for more detail, but basically if you want to create a verb that might perform an action to something, and possibly have a further action occur, then the form would be:

```
@verb object:<verb to create> <direct object> <preposition>
<indirect object>
```

For our purposes, though, we just want to play the piano, which is the direct object, so the form using **this**, referring to the piano, would be necessary. Here it is again, with the message the system gives upon execution:

```
@verb #8636:play this
Verb added (0).
```

Now to actually type in the programming code, you can use a built-in editor available on the MOO. Type in the **@edit** command, the object, a colon and the verb to be edited:

```
@edit piano:play
```

It's basically the same line editor used for internal MOOmail. Lines in mail messages require the **say** command (substitute a quote mark ["]) on each line:

```
Now editing #8636:play.
```

Type in the first line. It tells the room to make a message for all to hear:

```
"player.location:announce("The piano plays Chopin's Ballade in f
minor.");
```

Press ENTER. The system will report:

```
Line 1 added.
```

Add the second line. It tells the player who typed *play piano* that something has happened:

```
"player:tell("The piano plays Chopin's Ballade in f minor.");
```

Press ENTER, and the system will report:

```
Line 2 added.
```

Now use the **compile** command to have the verb's programming validated and activated for the object:

```
compile
```

If you receive the following report:

```
#8636:play successfully compiled.
```

you've made no errors and the system accepts the verb. It will not happen on the first try. The editor is difficult to use. You may want to edit off-line in some text editor you know better and then paste in your commands. This won't work in all cases, however. (For instance, DOS treats certain text codes, such as ends of lines, differently than UNIX, which may cause problems.) If errors persist, you may have to resort to using the MOO editor. Keep at it.

If success is elusive, in MediaMOO type the command:

```
@page help with <question>
```

and someone in the know will try to help.

Now, to test the verb we made, type:

```
play piano
```

The system reports:

```
"The piano plays Chopin's Ballade in f minor."
```

Now type in some suitable celebratory:

```
yahoo.
```

You did it yourself.

Chapter 8

Issues

Commerce

there are ongoing explorations to gauge how the interactive aspect of the global Internet might be used to further commerce. Much has been made, and will be made, of the anti-commercial mindset of many Net denizens. The violent reaction to an incident in which a pair of lawyers posted an ad for their services on all of the thousands of Usenet newsgroups has received a lot of attention. The lawyers' e-mail box was flooded with hate mail, death threats, and just plain junk, and the system they used was disrupted to the point that their account was removed until they threatened to sue. An obvious misuse, but the lawyers got lots of clients, and though calling them pioneers would be a stretch, the potential for advertising was clearly demonstrated. The Net will, as everything else does, come into the service of commerce. Compare the reaction of the incensed network crowd to the following quote:

> "You have debased [my] child. You have made him a laughingstock of intelligence...a stench in the nostrils of the gods of the ionosphere."

That was Dr. Lee De Forest in a speech to the National Association of Broadcasters, concerning what they had done with his innovation, the technology that eventually became television (Microsoft Bookshelf, 1994). These days, the common term for a comment like that would be *flame*.

In a way, the network will survive and prosper only if it can lash itself to a productive economic role. Until recently, it survived mostly on the largesse made possible by research money and academic support. The National Science Foundation, however, has cut it loose.

The first attempts at commercial MUD methodology will point the way. Writer/lecturer Chris Hand describes an event he helped organize:

> "You may be interested in the event we just had.... It was an online virtual Trade Exhibition—we believe the first event of its kind. Paying exhibitors had stands in a virtual exhibition hall, with representatives of the companies logging in to 'man' the stands. Robots were provided to help/stand in and to give out leaflets.
>
> The event was implemented using a MOO which we hacked to support connections over the World Wide Web. Anyone on the Internet could register as a 'virtual delegate,' and once they'd done so they could connect to his or her own personal Web page (effectively the Web view of his or her virtual persona) to browse any brochures, business cards, etc., that they'd been given.
>
> The event, known as TaTTOO'95 On-line, was run in conjunction with TaTTOO'95, an annual (real-life) conference on 'Teaching and Training in Object Technology' held at De Montfort University in Leicester, England. TaTTOO'95 On-line was supported by IBM, which provided a machine and network connection at their site in Portsmouth, England."

For showing and marketing, the network can, and will, be utilized to great effect. For money to change hands online though, as it does in the real-life streams of commerce, there must be more confidence that the money sent (in the form of credit card purchases or some other wired transaction) will arrive safely at its intended destination.

Meeting Space™—Business in the MUD

Jon Callas, director of technology at World Benders, Inc., doesn't see hack-and-slash when he sees a MUD, but sees an opportunity for a ground-breaking medium in which to conduct or augment a business conference. Meeting Space is his idea of a commerce-enhancing application of the multi-user environment.

"People are using it. Our clients include Apple, GTE and some small consulting firms," says Callas. What they are using are text-and-graphics-shared environments which can be installed on a company host computer. The users can then dial in or link up through an existing LAN or WAN to the MUD environment to conduct business. Often Meeting Space is used as a tool to enhance a conference call. It's also possible to attend a Meeting Space Meeting via the Internet.

There is a graphical front-end client which includes icons and a text box. A Meeting Space MUD runs on a Macintosh under Appletalk. Through it the participants can conduct slide shows, as well as store, present and transfer documents. It's a way of personalizing—and making interactive—often dry corporate communications and data exchange.

There are plans for an audio feature, including voice, and the long-term plan is to eventually incoporate desktop video. "The response has been good. And new users would find it easy to use. If you've worked with a word processor and e-mail, you can use Meeting Space."

If the "virtual corporation" is one of the more ethereal of business trends, Callas's product may be one way to give it form.

For information on Meeting Space, e-mail a request to:

wb-info@worldbenders.com

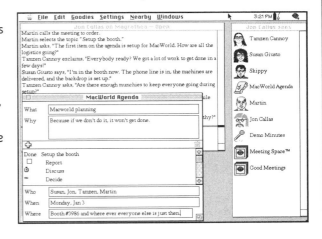

Security

The more users and systems on the Net, the more porous it will become. The basic technology (the data interchange protocols) remains relatively static, but the growing population brings with it an increase in people who want to do mischief. Decent, nondisruptive users have the same effect as they always do, no matter what their numbers.

A recent eruption of concern surrounded the revelation—subject of a *New York Times* front page story in January 1995—that it was possible to exploit long-hidden security holes in the TCP/IP system and do serious damage. A malevolent cracker could hijack outright a user's entire interactive session from across the network. In other words, picture yourself telnetting to a MUD sometime, when all of a sudden strange messages and text appear on the screen and nothing you type has any effect. It seems like you've lost control. In fact, you have. Your connection has been seized by someone who has found a way to forge the addresses each little packet of data carries with it. The computer to which you are telnetting does not know the difference. It is receiving packets that are, apparently, addressed properly.

The technique is called "packet spoofing" and CERT, the Computer Emergency Response Team, which tracks such occurrences, issued an advisory about it: "In taking over the existing connections, intruders can bypass one-time passwords and other strong authentication schemes by tapping the connection after the authentication is complete. For example, a legitimate user connects to a remote site through a login or terminal session; the intruder hijacks the connection after the user has completed the authentication to the remote location; the remote site is now compromised."

The advisory identifies routing hardware and configurations that are vulnerable and then lists some signs that systems administrators can communicate to alert their users—such as strange text or inexplicably blank screens. Besides that, nothing can be done to protect systems that don't take proper measures, and even some that do. The holes had been long known, and their late exploitation is a sign that other, more easily breached holes have been sealed. But the TCP/IP system of communication was designed at an earlier time, when Net attacks were rare, and the network was more open and trusting. That time is past.

Art

And, finally, what does it all mean for the creative individual? Are there new forms of expression emerging that are more immediate and fluid, less frozen and static than current forms?

To see how the fantasy role-players frolic and churn out the text you might think you walked into a Tolkien volume come to life. The sheer number of fantasy-themed MUDs, though, and all the stock blathering about "the gods of old" belies any notion that the endeavor is creative, lending credence to the dismissive viewpoint that it's all "hobby." The gamers don't take kindly to this opinion, of course. In business computer circles, to be called a "game" is equivalent to a quick death. This will soon change, as well.

Games come in many forms, and simulation is one of them. A networking researcher on the forefront of the search for high-speed technology once mused that there was no real potential for the idea of "movies on-demand," the most common rationalization for all the recent Net hype. No, the most likely economically justifiable use for such a network would be to simulate real-time business crisis situations for high-level corporate personnel. In other words, the high-speed networks will be a toy for corporate fat cats. On them, they will be playing a game, though you can be sure they will never be labeled as such.

Is it a new form of fiction writing, a real-time playacting of dialogue and actions on the fly? The consensus of a group of computers-in-writing teachers to whom that question was posed was that no, what they were doing while horsing around in the MUDs was not fiction, it was real, even though, nearly without exception, they were all presenting behind made-up names and created—either partially or totally—personae.

More encouraging are those MUD system admins who look upon the MUD as a medium on which to assert their own artistic sensibilities and then launch their worlds so that others can be set loose in them. There are godlike delusions in all such administrators, as their godlike designations for themselves readily illustrate, but those who seek to apply unusual themes to their MUDs—the Aztec/Turkic-themed Gohs MUD, featured in an earlier chapter, is an example—might just constitute a dynamic text creation akin to a work of fiction. The rumored Wild West and Egypt MUDs, which have yet to appear (the creators assure me they're still under construction), would be others. These efforts give those who sense the emergence of a new form of expression more hope. General recognition of such developments is a long way off. As mentioned in an earlier section, this period in the network's time line may be regarded as a sort of Iron Age. The tools are spreading, but there's a lot of development yet to go.

As a way of passing pure information, the usefulness of the Net is undeniable. The World Wide Web, with its hypertext connective ease-of-use and graphics (when used with suitable client software), is emerging as the most attractive and efficient way to pass information yet devised. It is not much different in that respect than the familiar forms it seems to use as models: the newspapers (efficient information transfer, relatively speaking) and magazines (attractive information transfer). The Web though, like those other models, is essentially a one-way affair, feeding a flow of interpretations from "homepage" creators to a consuming public. There is less gatekeeping than in the press—fewer editors—but there is still no give and take. (Plenty of forms to fill out though.)

MUDs and IRC, on the other hand, are unpredictable and lifelike. There's dynamic interplay, ideas discussed "face to face," politics, love, death, conflict and concordance. If the Web is destined to be the outward face of this distributed network beast, then the multiple-user landscapes, the MUDs, are destined to be its soul.

Appendix A

Table of Contents

Related Usenet Newsgroups

A few IRC-related newsgroups:

alt.irc
alt.irc.announce
alt.irc.questions

Some MUD newsgroups:

alt.mud
alt.mud.bsx
alt.mud.lp
alt.mud.moo
alt.mudders.anonymous
rec.games.mud.admin
rec.game.mud.announce
rec.games.mud.diku
rec.games.mud.lp
rec.games.mud.misc
rec.games.mud.tiny

World Wide Web

The two best starting points for Web wanderings on subjects in this book would be those below. One characteristic of the Web is you don't need more than one good starting point before you quickly find yourself nearly drowning in information.

Lydia Leong's MUD resource:

```
http://www.cis.upenn.edu/~lwl/mudinfo.html
```

Internet Relay Chat:

```
http://alpha.acast.nova.edu/irc.html
```

MUD FAQ

Following is an excerpt from Jennifer Smith's Frequently Asked Questions (FAQ) file on MUDs. This is Part 2—Clients and Servers (published with permission). For those with the resources, know-how, and desire to put up a MUD or a client to access one, here's some of what you need to know:

```
FAQ #2/3: MUD Clients and Servers
From: Jennifer "Moira" Smith <jds@math.okstate.edu>
Date: 16 Jan 1995 07:00:58 GMT

Archive-name: games/mud-faq/part2

              FREQUENTLY ASKED QUESTIONS: MUD CLIENTS AND SERVERS


Table of Contents

      * Client Information
          + 2.1. What is a client?
          + 2.2. Where do I get clients?
          + 2.3. What operating systems do clients run on?
          + 2.4. Is there anything wrong with running a client?
          + 2.5. What different clients are available? [Client List]
      * Glossary of Client terms
      * Server Information
          + 2.6. What is a server?
          + 2.7. Where do I get servers?
          + 2.8. What operating systems to servers run on?
          + 2.9. Is there anything wrong with running a server?
          + 2.10. What different servers are available? [Server List]
      * General Information
          + 2.11. What do I do if my client/server won't compile?
          + 2.12. Should I read the documentation of whatever client or
                     server I select?
          + 2.13. What is FTP, and how do I use it?

  CLIENT INFORMATION

  2.1. What is a client?

  Clients are programs, usually written in C, that connect up to
  servers. Telnet is one such client program. Many clients written for
  MUDs have special added bonus features through which they filter the
  output; most, for instance, separate your input line from the output
  lines and wraps words after 80 columns. Some also have a macro-
  writing capability which allows the user to execute several commands
  with just a few keypresses. Some allow you to highlight output coming
  from certain players or suppress it altogether. Still other clients
  make the sometimes tedious task of building new areas a breeze.
```

2.2. Where do I get clients?

Listed below is a list of clients, and a site or two where they can be
ftped from. If the site is down, your best bet is to ask around. In
general, ftp.tcp.com and ftp.math.okstate.edu are good places to look.
Directions for how to ftp and unarchive clients are at the end of this
FAQ.

2.3. What operating systems do clients run on?

Most use BSD Unix, although many also run under SysV Unix. Some run
under VMS with either MultiNet or Wollongong networking, a few new
ones run on a Macintosh, and there's even one for IBM VM.

2.4. Is there anything wrong with running a client?

Not usually. Clients can be large when compiled, especially if they
have lots of nifty features. They don't take up much CPU time at all.
It is recommended that you ask your friendly systems administrator or
other machine-responsible person if it's okay for you to install one
on the system, if only for the reason that someone else might already
have done so, and you might be able to save space by sharing with
them. If there's a no games policy at your site, don't try to sneak by
it with a client — their activities are easily detectable. Be good.

2.5. What different clients are available?

Here's a reasonably accurate listing of available clients. Please note
that I have not tested each of these, and they're not guaranteed to
work for you. If your favorite client isn't listed here, please drop a
short note describing the client's features and where it can be ftp'd
from to jds@math.okstate.edu.

The following clients are detailed below. Directions for how to ftp
and unarchive clients and servers can be found at the end of this FAQ.

Unix Clients
        TinyTalk, TinyFugue, TclTT, VT, LPTalk, SayWat, PMF, TinyView,
        TinTin, TinTin++, TUsh, LPmudr

Emacs Clients
        MUD.el, TinyTalk.el, LPmud.el, CLPmud.el, MyMud.el

VMS Clients
        tfVMS, TINT, TINTw, DINK, FooTalk

Misc Clients
        REXXTALK, MUDDweller, Mudling, MUDCaller, BSXMUD Clients

---

TinyTalk
        Runs on BSD or SysV. Latest version is 1.1.7GEW. Designed

primarily for TinyMUD-style muds. Features include line editing, command history, hiliting (whispers, pages, and users), gag, auto-login, simple macros, logging, and cyberportals.

ftp.math.okstate.edu:/pub/muds/clients/UnixClients
parcftp.xerox.com:/pub/MOO/clients
ftp.tcp.com:/pub/mud/Clients

TinyFugue

Runs on BSD or SysV. Latest version is 3.2beta4. Commonly known as 'tf.' Designed primarily for TinyMUD-style muds, although will run on LPMUDs and Dikus. Features include regexp hilites and gags, auto-login, macros, line editing, screen mode, triggers, cyberportals, logging, file and command uploading, shells, and multiple connects.

ftp.math.okstate.edu:/pub/muds/clients/UnixClients/tf
ftp.tcp.com:/pub/mud/Clients

TclTT   Runs on BSD. Latest version is 0.9. Designed primarily for TinyMUD-style muds. Features include regexp hilites, regexp gags, logging, auto-login, partial file uploading, triggers, and programmability.
ftp.white.toronto.edu:/pub/muds/tcltt
ftp.math.okstate.edu:/pub/muds/clients/UnixClients

VT   Runs on BSD or SysV. Latest version is 2.15. Must have vt102 capabilities. Useable for all types of muds. Features include a C-like extension language (VTC) and a simple windowing system.

ftp.math.okstate.edu:/pub/muds/clients/vt
ftp.tcp.com:/pub/mud/Clients

LPTalk

Runs on BSD or SysV. Latest version is 1.2.1. Designed primarily for LPMUDs. Features include hiliting, gags, auto-login, simple macros, logging.

ftp.math.okstate.edu:/pub/muds/clients/UnixClients

SayWat

Runs on BSD. Latest version is 0.30beta. Designed primarily for TinyMUD-style muds. Features include regexp hilites, regexp gags, macros, triggers, logging, cyberportals, rudimentary xterm support, command line history, multiple connects, and file uploading.

ftp.math.okstate.edu:/pub/muds/clients/UnixClients

PMF   Runs on BSD. Latest version is 1.13.1. Usable for both LPMUDs and TinyMUD-style muds. Features include line editing, auto-login, macros, triggers, gags, logging, file uploads, an X-window interface, and ability to do Sparc sounds.

```
        ftp.lysator.liu.se:/pub/lpmud/clients
        ftp.math.okstate.edu:/pub/muds/clients/UnixClients
```

TinyView
        Runs on BSD. Latest version is 1.0. Designed for use primarily
        for TinyMUD-style muds. Features include screen mode, macros,
        history buffers, line editing, and multiple connects.
        NO KNOWN SITE

TinTin
        Runs on BSD. Latest version is 2.0. Designed primarily for
        Dikus. Features include macros, triggers, tick-counter
        features, and multiple connects.

```
        ftp.math.okstate.edu:/pub/muds/clients/UnixClients
```

TinTin++
        Runs on BSD or SysV. Latest version is 1.5pl5. Derived and
        improved from TinTin. Additional features include variables,
        faster triggers, and a split screen mode.

```
        ftp.princeton.edu:/pub/tintin++/dist
        ftp.math.okstate.edu:/pub/muds/clients/UnixClients
```

TUsh   Runs on BSD or SysV. Latest version is 1.74. Features include
        hiliting, triggers, aliasing, history buffer, and screen mode.
        ftp.math.okstate.edu:/pub/muds/clients/UnixClients

LPmudr
        Runs on BSD or SysV. Latest version is 2.7. Designed primarily
        for LPMUDs. Features include line editing, command history,
        auto-login and logging.

```
        ftp.math.okstate.edu:/pub/muds/clients/UnixClients
```

MUD.el
        Runs on GNU Emacs. Usable for TinyMUD-style muds, LPMUDs, and
        MOOs. Features include auto-login, macros, logging,
        cyberportals, screen mode, and it is programmable.

```
        parcftp.xerox.com:/pub/MOO/clients
        ftp.math.okstate.edu:/pub/muds/clients/UnixClients
```

TinyTalk.el
        Runs on GNU Emacs. Latest version is 0.5. Designed primarily
        for TinyMUD-style muds. Features include auto-login, macros,
        logging, screen mode, and it is programmable.

```
        ftp.tcp.com(128.95.10.106):/pub/mud/Clients
        ftp.math.okstate.edu:/pub/muds/clients/UnixClients
```

LPmud.el
        Runs on GNU Emacs. Designed primarily for LPMUDs. Features

include macros, triggers, file uploading, logging, screen mode, and it is programmable.

```
ftp.lysator.liu.se:/pub/lpmud/clients
ftp.math.okstate.edu:/pub/muds/clients/UnixClients
```

CLPmud.el
Runs on GNU Emacs. Designed primarily for LPMUDs. Similar to LPmud.el, but with the added capability for remote file retrieval, editing in emacs, and saving, for LPMud wizards.

```
mizar.docs.uu.se:/pub/lpmud
```

MyMud.el
Runs on GNU Emacs. Latest version is 1.31. Designed primarily for LPMUDs and Dikus. Features include screen mode, auto-login, macros, triggers, autonavigator, and it is programmable.

```
ftp.math.okstate.edu:/pub/muds/clients/UnixClients
ftp.tcp.com:/pub/mud/Clients
```

tfVMS   VMS version of TinyFugue (see above). Uses Wollongong networking. Latest version is 1.0b2.

```
ftp.math.okstate.edu:/pub/muds/clients/VMSClients
```

TINT   Runs on VMS with MultiNet networking. Latest version is 2.2. Designed primarily for TinyMUD-style muds. Features include hiliting (whispers, pages, users), gags, file uploading, simple macros, screen mode. See also TINTw.

```
ftp.math.okstate.edu:/pub/muds/clients/VMSClients
```

TINTw   Runs on VMS with Wollongong networking. See TINT.

```
ftp.math.okstate.edu:/pub/muds/clients/VMSClients
ftp.tcp.com:/pub/mud/Clients
```

DINK   Runs on VMS with either Wollongong or MultiNet networking. Similar to TINT. No longer supported by the author.

```
ftp.math.okstate.edu:/pub/muds/clients/VMSClients
ftp.tcp.com:/pub/mud/Clients
```

FooTalk
Runs on VMS with MultiNet networking and BSD Unix. Primarily designed for TinyMUD-style muds. Features include screen mode, and it is programmable. See RispTalk below.

```
ftp.math.okstate.edu:/pub/muds/clients/VMSClients

ftp.math.okstate.edu:/pub/muds/clients/UnixClients
```

REXXTALK
 Runs on IBM VM. Latest version is 2.1. Designed primarily for
 TinyMUD-style muds. Features include screen mode, logging,
 macros, triggers, hilites, gags, and auto-login. Allows some
 IBM VM programs to be run while connected to a foreign host,
 such as TELL and MAIL.

 ftp.math.okstate.edu:/pub/muds/clients/misc

MUDDweller
 Runs on any Macintosh. Latest version is 1.2. Connects to a MUD
 through either the communications toolbox or by MacTCP. Usable
 for both LPMUDs and TinyMUD-style muds. Current features
 include multiple connections, a command history and a built-in
 MTP client for LPMUDs.

 rudolf.ethz.ch:/pub/mud

 mac.archive.umich.edu:/mac/util/comm
 ftp.tcp.com:/pub/mud/Clients

Mudling
 Runs on any Macintosh. Latest version is 0.9b26. Features
 include multiple connections, triggers, macros, command line
 history, separate input and output windows, and a rudimentary
 mapping system.

 imv.aau.dk:/pub/Mudling
 ftp.math.okstate.edu:/pub/muds/clients/misc

MUDCaller
 Runs under MS-DOS. Latest version is 2.50. Requires an Ethernet
 card, and uses the Crynwr Packet drivers. Does NOT work with a
 modem. (If you telnet in MS-DOS, you can probably use this.)
 Features include multiple connections, triggers, command-line
 history, scrollback, logging, macros, and separate input and
 output windows.

 ftp.tcp.com:/pub/mud/Clients
 ftp.math.okstate.edu:/pub/muds/clients/misc
 oak.oakland.edu:/pub/msdos/pktdrvr

BSXMUD Clients
 These clients run on various platforms, and allow the user to
 be able to see the graphics produced by BSXMUDs. BSXMUDs are
 generally LPMUDs (but not necessarily) who have been hacked to
 enable the sending of polygon graphics coordinates to
 BSXclients, thus letting you play a graphic MUD instead of just
 a text-based one. For more information, contact
 vexar@watserv.ucr.edu.

 For Amiga: modem or TCP/IP - AmigaBSXClient2_2.lha
 For PC: requires a modem - msclient.lzh AND x00v124.zip
 For X11: sources, version 3.2 - bsxclient3_8c.tar.Z
 For Sun4: binary - client.sparc.tar.Z

Also available are programs to custom-draw your own graphics

for a BSXMUD: - muddraw.tar.gz, bsxdraw.zoo

ftp.lysator.liu.se:pub/lpmud/bsx
ftp.math.okstate.edu:/pub/muds/BSXstuff

GLOSSARY OF CLIENT TERMS

Auto-login
Automatically logs into the game for you.

Hiliting
Allows boldface or other emphasis to be applied to some text. Often allowed on particular types of output (e.g. whispers), or particular players. "Regexp" means that UNIX-style regular expressions can be used to select text to hilite.

Gag
Allows some text to be suppressed. The choice of what to suppress is often similar to hiliting (players or regular expressions).

Macros
Allows new commands to be defined. How complex a macro can be varies greatly between clients; check the documentation for details.

Logging
Allows output from the MUD to be recorded in a file.

Cyberportals
Supports special MUD features which can automatically reconnect you to another MUD server.

Screen Mode
Supports some sort of screen mode (beyond just scrolling your output off the top of the screen) on some terminals. The exact support varies.

Triggers
Supports events which happen when certain actions on the MUD occur (e.g. waving when a player enters the room). (This can nearly always be trivially done on programmable clients, even if it isn't built in.)

Programmable
Supports some sort of client-local programming. Read the documentation.

Some of these clients are more featured than others, and some require a fair degree of computer literacy. TinyTalk and TinyFugue are among the easiest to learn; Tcltt and VT are more professional. Caveat Emptor. Since many MUDders write their own clients, this list can never be complete. As above, ask around.

SERVER INFORMATION

2.6. What is a server?

A server is a program which accepts connections, receives data, mulls it over, and sends out some output. In the MUD world, the server keeps track of the database, the current players, the rules, and sometimes the time (or the heartbeat). Servers are usually very large C programs which maintain a small-to-enormous database of the objects, rooms, players and miscellany of the MUD.

2.7. Where do I get servers?

Below (see question 2.10)there is a list of different types of servers, complete with ftp sites on which they can be found. Be aware that this list is far from complete, as new servers pop up constantly, and the existing ones are still being developed.

2.8. What operating systems do servers run on?

Most servers require some form of UNIX, be it BSD or SysV. A few servers are being ported to VMS nowadays, and there are a few which have versions for MS-DOS and Amigas.

2.9. Is there anything wrong with running a server?

Because of their size and their constant computational activities, servers can be extremely CPU-intensive and can even be crippling to any other work done on that computer. Even if they're not CPU-intensive, most MUDs can take up a fair amount of disk space - anywhere from 10 to 90 megs, which could impact the other users on the machine. Do not ever run a MUD server on a machine illicitly or without express permission from the person responsible for the machine. Many universities and companies have strict policies about that sort of behavior which you don't want to cross.

Of course, people who don't know any better start up illicit MUDs all the time. Apart from the possibility of losing all your work and energy to one press of a sysadmin's finger, there's no harm done to the player. But we must stress: running a MUD where you shouldn't can get you into a whole new world of hurt. Don't take the chance, it's not worth it.

2.10. What different servers are available?

There are probably as many MUD server types as there are MUDs. Since
everyone has his own opinions as to what MUDs should be like, and
since the server source can be edited, most MUDs have site-specific
fixtures in them. However, there are a few main protoMUDs (also called
'vanilla versions' because they haven't been 'flavored' yet). Note
that this list is not complete, and that it may contain errors in fact
or judgement, but is deemed pretty much right as of this writing.
Corrections/additions to jds@math.okstate.edu are welcomed.

There are essentially three groups of muds:
    * Combat-oriented MUDs (LP/Diku/etc)
    * TinyMUD and its direct descendants, aka social-oriented MUDs
    * Miscellaneous

The majority of the muds in the miscellaneous category are not
combat-oriented muds at all, and indeed many take after TinyMUD in
most things. However, as these muds are not a direct derivative of the
original TinyMUD code, I've stuck them in their own category. The
authors listed for each server are very probably not the people
currently working on that code. To find out who's currently in charge
of the code, either ftp the latest version and look for a README file,
or ask around.

A note on the term combat-oriented: this generally means that combat
is an inherent part of the culture of the mud. A flight-simulator
could be called a combat-oriented game, just as truly as your typical
shoot-em-up game could be. A social-oriented mud has a different
focus, one dependent either on role-playing social interactions (which
MAY include combat!), or on not role-playing at all, but merely talking
with friends or other such benign things. It should be emphasized that
simply because a given server is listed in the combat-oriented area,
it does not necessarily follow that it must be a combat-oriented
MUD. Most servers are fairly flexible, and can be used for social and
combat uses alike, as well as for business and education.

Detailed listings of the following servers are below. Directions for
how to ftp and unarchive servers can be found at the end of this FAQ.

Combat-Oriented MUDs
        MUD, AberMUD, LPMUD, DGD, DikuMUD, KMUD, YAMA, UriMUD, Ogham,
        CircleMUD, AmigaMUD

Social-Oriented MUDs
        TinyMUD, TinyMUCK v1.*, TinyMUSH, TinyMUCK v2.*, TinyMUSE,
        TinyMAGE, MUG, TeenyMUD

Misc MUDs
        UberMUD, MOO, LambdaMOO, SMUG, UnterMUD

Combat-Oriented MUDs

MUD   The original, by Richard Bartle and Roy Trubshaw, written back
        in 1978. An advanced version of MUD2 is now running on
        CompuServe under the name of "British Legends." A MUD2 can be
        found running at mud.almac.co.uk. Source generally not
        available.

AberMUD
        One of the first adventure-based MUDs. Players cannot build. In
        later versions, a class system was added, and wizards can build
        onto the database. It's named after the university at which it
        was written, Aberystwyth. Latest version is 5.21.5. Supports
        all the usual in-combat game design, including BSX graphics and
        MudWHO. Not too big, and it will run under BSD and SYSV. Amiga
        TCP/IP support now included.
        Author, contact address, and mailing list address is
        A.Cox@swan.ac.uk.

        sunacm.swan.ac.uk:/pub/misc/AberMUD5/SOURCE

LPMUD   The most popular combat-oriented MUD. Players cannot build. Be
        warned, though: LPMUD servers version 3.* themselves are very
        generic - all of the universe rules and so forth are written in
        a separate module, called the mudlib. Most LPMUDs running are
        written to be some sort of combat system, which is why I've
        classified them here, but they don't have to be! Wizards can
        build onto the database, by means of an object-oriented C-like
        internal language called LP-C. It's named after its primary
        author, Lars Penjl. Latest version is 3.2, aka Amylaar. Fairly
        stable, and size varies from medium to large. Driver (server)
        versions seem to have split into several main variants, not
        counting possible mudlibs (databases) available. Amylaar, CD,
        and MudOS are the current favorites. For further information,
        email to amylaar@meolyon.hanse.de.
        There is a port of 3.1.2 for Amigas, called amud, now included
        in LPMUD v3.2. For further information email to
        mateese@ibr.cs.tu-bs.de.
        See the rec.games.mud.lp FAQ for more info.

        ftp.lysator.liu.se:/pub/lpmud
        ftp.cd.chalmers.se:/pub/lpmud/cdlib
        ftp.tu-bs.de:/pub/games/lpmud
        ftp.ccs.neu.edu:/pub/mud/drivers/mudos

        There is a port of 3.1.2 for MS-DOS, that requires at least a
        '386 to run. It accepts connections from serial ports.

        ftp.ccs.neu.edu:/pub/mud/drivers/lpmud/msdos

DGD   A reimplementation from scratch of the LPMUD server. It is
        disk-based, and thus uses less memory. It's also smaller and
        lacks many of the featuers of the other LPMUD servers, though
        it is capable of simulating most of those features in LPC.

There is no mudlib specifically for DGD yet, although there are some MUDs that use DGD to simulate an LP variant. The name stands for Dworkin's Game Driver. Mostly stable. Has been ported to Atari ST and Commodore Amiga.

ftp.lysator.liu.se:/pub/lpmud/drivers/dgd

DikuMUD

Newer than LPMud, and gaining in popularity. Almost identical from the players' point of view. Uses a guild system instead of a straight class system. Wizards can add on to the database, but there is no programming language, as in LP. It's named after the university at which it was written, Datalogisk Institut Koebenhavns Universitet (Dept. of Datalogy, University of Copenhagen).

coyote.cs.wmich.edu:/pub/Games/DikuMUD

KMUD   Still under development. KMUD is similar to LPMUD in feel, but only runs on PCs. It does have some on line building commands. It accepts connections from serial ports (requires a FOSSIL driver), and through TCP/IP telnet protocol.

NO KNOWN SITE

YAMA   PC mud writing system, using waterloo wattcp. Runs on a 640K PC/XT or better. Runs best with about a 1Mb ram disk, but is fine without. A separate windows version (yamaw) runs under windows and allows you to run a mud on a 286 or higher without taking over the machine.

sunacm.swan.ac.uk:/pub/misc/YAMA

UriMUD

Developed from an LPMud2.4.5, the code structure is very similar. Features include better speed, flexibility, stronger LPC, and the ability to handle multiple mudlibs under one parser. Latest version is 2.5.

ftp.netcom.com:/pub/urimud

Ogham   From the players' point of view, similar to LPMUD. No programming language or database, as mud compiles to a single binary executable.

ftp.ccs.neu.edu:/pub/mud/servers/ogham
ftp.math.okstate.edu:/pub/muds/servers

CircleMUD

Derivative of DikuMUD Gamma v0.0. Developed by Jeremy Elson (jelson@cs.jhu.edu). Less buggy and tighter code all in all. Latest version is 2.20. Also see URL

```
http://www.cs.jhu.edu/other/jelson/circle.html

ftp.cs.jhu.edu:/pub/CircleMUD
sunsite.unc.edu:/pub/Linux/games/muds
ftp.math.okstate.edu:/pub/muds/servers
```

AmigaMUD
        Written by scratch for Commodore Amiga computers. Includes
        custom client which supports graphics and sound. Disk-based,
        fast programming language, standard scenario including built-in
        mail and boards. Obtained from the Aminet ftp sites.

```
ftp.wustl.edu:/pub/aminet/game/role/AMClnt.lha, AMSrv.lha
```

   TinyMUD-style MUDs

TinyMUD
        The first, and archetypical, socially-oriented MUD. It was
        inspired by and looks like the old VMS game Monster, by Rich
        Skrenta. Players can explore and build, with the basic @dig,
        @create, @open, @link, @unlink, @lock commands. Players cannot
        teleport, and couldn't use @chown or set things DARK until
        later versions. Recycling didn't exist till the later versions,
        either. It's called 'Tiny' because it is - compared to the
        combat-oriented MUDs. Original code written by Jim Aspnes. Last
        known version is 1.5.5. Not terribly big, and quite stable.

```
ftp.math.okstate.edu:/pub/muds/servers
primerd.prime.com:/pub/games/mud/tinymud
```

        There is a PC port of TinyMUD, along with some extra code. It
        accepts connections from serial ports.

```
ftp.tcp.com:/pub/mud/TinyMUD
```

        There is a modified version of TinyMUD called PRISM, that works
        for PCs, Atari STs, and most Unixes. It also comes with an
        internal BSX client for MSDOS.

```
lister.cc.ic.ac.uk:/pub/prism
```

TinyMUCK v1.*
        The first derivative from TinyMUD. Identical to TinyMUD, except
        that it added the concept of moveable exits, called @actions.
        Also introduced the JUMP_OK flag, which allows players to use
        @teleport, and @recycle, which TinyMUD later added. Its name,
        MUCK, is derived from MUD, and means nothing in particular.
        Original code written by Stephen White. Latest stable verion is
        1.2.c&r, which brought TinyMUCKv1 up to date with later TinyMUD
        things. Not terribly big.

```
ftp.math.okstate.edu:/pub/muds/servers
```

TinyMUSH

The second derivative from TinyMUD. Also identical to TinyMUD, with the addition of a very primitive script-like language. Introduced JUMP_OK like TinyMUCK, and has recycling, except it is called @destroy. Also introduced the concept of PUPPETs, and other objects that can listen. In later versions the script language was extended greatly, adding math functions and many database functions. In the latest version, 2.0.*, it's gone to a disk-basing system as well. Its name, MUSH, stands for Multi-User Shared Hallucination. Original code written by Larry Foard. The latest non- disk-based version is PennMUSH1.50p10, which is quite similar to 2.0 from the user's point of view. Both the disk-based version and the non-disk-based version are being developed at the same time. TinyMUSH is more efficient in some ways than TinyMUD, but winds up being larger because of programmed objects. Version 2.0 in general uses less memory but a great deal more disk space. 2.0 may also be able to be run under VMS, as well as both BSD and SysV UNIX. Most recent version is 2.0.10p6.

```
caisr2.caisr.cwru.edu:/pub/mush
ftp.cis.upenn.edu:/pub/lwl
primerd.prime.com:/pub/games/mud/tinymush
ftp.tcp.com:/pub/mud/TinyMUSH
```

TinyMUCK v2.*

TinyMUCKv1.* with a programming language added. The language, MUF (multiple user forth), is only accessible to people with the MUCKER flag. Changed the rules of the JUMP_OK flag somewhat, to where it's nice and confusing now. MUF is very powerful, and can do just about anything a wizard can. Original version 2.* code written by Lachesis. Latest version is 2.3b, with several varieties (FBMUCK and DaemonMUCK 0.14 the most common). The name doesn't mean anything. Can be quite large, especially with many programs. Mostly stable.

```
ftp.tcp.com:/pub/mud/TinyMUCK
```

TinyMUSE

A derivative of TinyMUSH. Many more script-language extensions and flags. Reintroduced a class system, a-la combat-oriented MUDs. The name stands for Multi-User Simulation Environment. Latest version is 1.7b4. Not very stable.

```
mcmuse.mc.maricopa.edu:/muse/server
caisr2.caisr.cwru.edu:/pub/mush/muse
```

TinyMAGE

The bastard son of TinyMUSH and TinyMUCK. It combines some of MUSH's concepts (such as puppets, @adesc/@asucc, several programming functions, and a few flags) with TinyMUCK2.x.

Interesting idea, really busted code. The name doesn't mean anything. Latest version is 1.1.2.

ftp.tcp.com:/pub/mud/TinyMAGE

MUG Derivative of TinyMUD 1.4.1. Its name stands for Multi-User Game. Powerful but awkward programming language, which is an extension of the user language; primitive notion of Puppets; inheritance; sane variable/property matching; arrays and dictionaries in hardcode. Somewhat non-standard and buggy in a few places.

Requires gcc.2.4.5 or greater (or other good C++ compiler) to compile. Available by e-mail from wizard@cs.man.ac.uk; development site is UglyMUG (wyrm.cs.man.ac.uk 6239).

TeenyMUD
A TinyMUD clone, written from scratch. Its main feature is that it is disk-based. Original code written by Andrew Molitor. Latest version is 1.3. Very small, and mostly stable.

fido.econ.arizona.edu:/pub/teeny

Miscellaneous

UberMUD
The first MUD where the universe rules is written totally in the internal programming language, U. The language is very C/pascal-like. The permissions system is tricky, and writing up every universe rule (commands and all) without having big security holes is a pain. But it's one of the most flexible muds in existance. Great for writing up neat toys. It's also disk-based. Original code written by Marcus J. Ranum. Latest version is 1.13. Small in memory, but can eat up disk space. Quite stable.

decuac.dec.com:/pub/mud
ftp.white.toronto.edu:/pub/muds/uber
ftp.math.okstate.edu:/pub/muds/servers

MOO An Object-Oriented MUD. Unfortunately, the first few versions weren't fully object oriented. Later versions fixed that problem. There is a C-like internal programming language, and it can be a bit tricky. Original code written by Stephen White. Last version is 2.0a.

NO KNOWN SITE

LambdaMOO

An offshoot of MOO. Added more functionality, many new features, and a great deal more stability, in a general rewrite of the code. This is the only version of MOO that is still being developed, by Pavel Curtis. Latest version is 1.7.7.

parcftp.xerox.com:/pub/MOO

SMUG   Also known as TinyMUD v2.0. It has an internal programming language, and it does have some inheritance. Surprisingly similar to MOO in some ways. SMUG stands for Small Multi-User Game. Original code written by Jim Aspnes.

ftp.tcp.com:/pub/mud/Smug

UnterMUD

A network-oriented MUD. It's disk-based, with a variety of db layers to choose from. An UnterMUD can connect directly to other UnterMUDs, and players can carry stuff with them when they tour the Unterverse. This can be a bit baffling to a new user, admittedly, but those people already familiar with the old cyberportals and how they work (invented way back with the original TinyMUD) will adjust to the new real cyberportals easily. There is both a primitive scripting language and much of the U language from UberMUD built in, as well as a combat system that can be compiled in if wanted. The parsing can be a bit odd, especially if you're used to the TinyMUD-style parser. Unter is also the only MUD that can run under BSD Unix, SysVr4 Unix, and VMS with MultiNet networking, with little to no hacking. Original code written by Marcus J. Ranum.
Latest version is 2.1. Small in memory, but can eat up a lot of disk space.

ftp.math.okstate.edu:/pub/muds/servers
decuac.dec.com:/pub/mud
ftp.tcp.com:pub/mud/UnterMUD

Note: just because we say something's available doesn't mean we have it. Please don't ask us; ask around for ftp sites that might have them, or try looking on ftp.tcp.com or ftp.math.okstate.edu.

MUDlist
339 World Internetted Multi-User Dimensions
Confirmed as "up" between 24 JAN 95 and 1 FEB 1995.

Directory Introduction
Remember: there are no borders on the big Net so the electronic locales below have been assembled without regard to foreign jurisdictions. Be prepared to encounter languages and customs that may be unfamiliar.

This list was compiled using all the online resources available, including the Doran MUDlist, Lydia Leong's List of Mushs, Axl's MUD List, the University of Minnesota gopher and the Delphi Internet MUD gopher. There are also some which appear in none of those places.

The Net is always changing. A site that was up at a certain time may no longer be running. There are no guarantees. Although the information below may have a half-life, so does the information in, say, the Encyclopedia Britannica. But nobody says that is a bad idea.

No differentiation as to MUD type has been made. All MUDs are worth a visit.

What follows may be the most concentrated accumulation of interesting cyberspace destinations yet compiled and committed to paper.

See you on the nets.

William J. "Bilsabub-Bones-Clortho-Exeter" Shefski
1 FEB 1995

MUD	Telnet Address
5th Dimension	GAUSS.IFM.LIU.SE 3000
Abyss IV	129.89.68.89 4000
ACER ISLE	cave.pg.md.us 2222
ACME mud	MUD.CC.GENESEO.EDU 9000

MUD	Telnet Address
Adamant	rm600.rbg.informatik.th-darmstadt.de 4711
Addicted	SUN1.GWENT.AC.UK 6666
aGeoFiNsaNitY	whit.org 4000
Alatia	aann.tyrell.net 3000
Albanian	FRED.INDSTATE.EDU 2150
Albion Mud	VEDA.IS 4000
AlexMUD	alexmud.stacken.kth.se 4000
Alice's MUD Cafe	desire.apana.org.au 4000
Altered Dimensions II	SPRUCE.EVANSVILLE.EDU 6250
AmberMUSH	a.cs.okstate.edu 5150
Ancient Anguish	END2.BEDROCK.COM 2222
Angalon	NEUROMANCER.TAMU.EDU 3011
AnimeMUCK	eith.biostr.washington.edu 2035
AnimeMUCK	TCP.COM 2035
AnotherMUD	spider.compart.fi 4000
ApexMUD	APEX.YORKU.CA 4201
Apocalypse IV	SAPPHIRE.GEO.WVU.EDU 4000
Armageddon	thrash.isca.uiowa.edu 7777
Aurora	aurora.etsiig.uniovi.es 3000
AustinMud	imv.aau.dk 4000
BabeMUD	TEACHING4.PHYSICS.OX.AC.UK 4001
BarrenRealms	liii.com 8000

continues

MUD	Telnet Address
BatMUD	bat.cs.hut.fi 23
Battle MUD	netra.geko.com.au 5001
Belior Rising	BRAZIL-NUT.ENMU.EDU 4301
BernieMUD	FWK098037.RES-HALL.NWU.EDU 671
BlueFacialMUD	dallet.channel1.com 1234
BooMOO	pinot.callamer.com 1234
Brazilian Dreams	RED_PANDA.TBYTE.COM 4201
BTech3056	BTECH.NETAXS.COM 3056
Budapest	PROMETHEUS.BSD.UCHICAGO.EDU 6789
CajunMUD	acc.mcneese.edu 8000
Callandor	hro5.ptf.hro.nl 5317
CamelotMUSH	CADMAN.CIT.BUFFALO.EDU 5440
CanDUM II	ITRCHQ.ITRC.ON.CA 2001
CaseusVeloxMOO	Freak.ORG 7777
CaveMUCK	cave.tcp.com 2283
Chaos	chaos.bga.com 4000
Chaos II (Realms of Chaos)	CHAOS2.COLORADO.EDU 3456
Chatter	hawking.u.washington.edu 6000
ChibaMOO	chiba.picosof.com 7777
Chomestoru	dfw.net 4000
City of Darkness	MELANDRA.CS.MAN.AC.UK 2000
CoffeeHouse	eleven.uccs.edu 2525
Conspiracy!	ALMOND.ENMU.EDU 1066

MUD	Telnet Address
Cross the Ages	TC0.CHEM.TUE.NL 6997
Crossed Swords	SHSIBM.SHH.FI 3000
Crystal Shard	shard.mhv.net 9000
CrystalMUSH	MOINK.NMSU.EDU 6886
CthulhuMUSH	blade.stc.housing.washington.edu 6250
Cybermush	TLALOC.CMS.DMU.AC.UK 6250
DarkCastle	foxtrot.rahul.net 6666
Darker Realms	WORF.TAMU.EDU 2000
DarkWind	darkwind.i-link.com 3000
Dawn of Immortals	immortal.ncsa.uiuc.edu 2000
Dawn Sisters	ARMS.GPS.CALTECH.EDU 9944
Death's Domain	cybernet.cse.fau.edu 9000
Deep Seas	A.CS.OKSTATE.EDU 6250
DeeperTrouble	alk.iesd.auc.dk 4242
Delusions	iglou.com 4999
DikuMUDI	Dorothy.ibmPCUG.CO.UK 4000
Dirt	alkymene.uio.no 6715
Discordia	astro1.panet.utoledo.edu 4201
Diversity University	MOO.DU.ORG 8888
Divination Web	BILL.MATH.UCONN.EDU 9393
Doggie Mush	ALADDIN.DATAFLUX.BC.CA 8888
DONUT MOO (K-12)	BIGBIRD.STARK.K12.OH.US 7777

continues

MUD	Telnet Address
Doom Mud	Neuromancer.HACKS.Arizona.EDU 4000
Dragon's Den	hellfire.dusers.drexel.edu 2222
Dragon's Kingdom	204.95.160.13 4898
DragonDawn	CASHEW.ENMU.EDU 2222
Dragonfire	typo.umsl.edu 3000
DragonMUD	satan.ucsd.edu 4201
Dragons Legends and Lore	TRIDENT.EE.FIT.EDU 9000
Dragonsfire	MOO.ESKIMO.COM 7777
DragonSpires *(Requires special client software.)*	boris.eden.com 7734
Druid Muck	moink.nmsu.edu 4201
DUMII	dum.ludd.luth.se 2001
Dune	des8.u-strasbg.fr 8888
Eastern Stories	CISPPC2.CIS.NCTU.EDU.TW 8000
Eclipse MUD	MUD.BSD.UCHICAGO.EDU 6715
Elements of Paradox	ELOF.ACC.IIT.EDU 6996
Elendor MUSH	DANA.UCC.NAU.EDU 1892
Elenium MUSH	omega.ru.ac.za 4201
ElephantMUD	radian.ee.ic.ac.uk 4444
Elite	XBYSE.NADA.KTH.SE 4000
Empire	EINSTEIN.PHYSICS.DREXEL.EDU 4000
EndorMUD	endor.byu.edu 5555
EnsemMUD	oldensun.imag.fr 4000

MUD	Telnet Address
Entropy	monsoon.weather.Brockport.EDU 7777
Eon	MCMUSE.MC.MARICOPA.EDU 8888
EverDark	ATOMIC.COM 3000
Evil in the Extreme	jcowan.reslife.okstate.edu 4000
(EVIL!)Mud	INTAC.COM 4201
EyeballMERC	phobos.cimtek.com 4444
Fantasia	betz.biostr.washington.edu 4201
Farside	zeus.atinc.com 3000
FieryMud	fiery.eushc.org 4000
Final Frontiers MOO	UGLY.MICROSERVE.NET 2499
First Light	GOLD.T-INFORMATIK.BA-STUTTGART.DE 3000
FlatEarth	neumann.cba.csuohio.edu 7719
Formosa	db82.csie.ncu.edu.tw 4000
Four Seasons MOO	albion.cs.man.ac.uk 7777
FranDUM II	MOUSSON.ENST.FR 2001
FredMUD	fred.indstate.edu 2150
Frontiers	seahorse.acs.brockport.edu 5555
FurryMUCK	SNCILS.SNC.EDU 8888
FurToonia	rtd.com 8888
Future Realms MUSH	fender.onramp.net 1701
Gates of Hell	voyager6.Stanford.EDU 6060

continues

MUD	Telnet Address
GateWay	IDIOT.ALFRED.EDU 6969
Genesis	hamal2.cs.chalmers.se 3011
Genocide	genocide.shsu.edu 2222
Global MUSH	LANCELOT.CIF.ROCHESTER.EDU 4201
GodsHome	thakhasis.solace.mh.se 3000
Gohs Mush	VALHALLA.ACUSD.EDU 9999
GrimneMUD	grimne.pvv.unit.no 4000
Guardians Mush	jive.rahul.net 4205
Hall of Fame	MARVIN.DF.LTH.SE 2000
Hari MUD	tc0.chem.tue.nl 6997
Harper'sTale	srcrisc.srce.hr 8888
Haven	IDRZ07.ETHZ.CH 1999
Hercules MUD	sunshine.eushc.org 3000
Hero of the Lance	mencius.technet.sg 5000
HertsMUD	brunel.herts.ac.uk 4000
Highlands	jedi.cis.temple.edu 9001
HoloMuck	COLLATZ.MCRCIM.MCGILL.EDU 5757
Holomud	sprawl.fc.net 7777
Hotel California	Neuromancer.HACKS.Arizona.EDU 6060
IgorMUD	IGOR.MTEK.CHALMERS.SE 1701
ImageCastle	FOGEY.STANFORD.EDU 4201
Imperial	SUPERGIRL.CS.HUT.FI 6969
Imperium Gothique	cc.joensuu.fi 4000

MUD	Telnet Address
Incarnations	LUMLEY.CAIS.COM 4201
Infinity	SIRIUS.NMT.EDU 6715
Inner Spiral MUSH:	INSPIRAL.IS.NET 6666
Island	TEACHING4.PHYSICS.OX.AC.UK 2092 or 2093
Ivory Tower	MARVIN.MACC.WISC.EDU 2000
JeenusTooMUD	HEEGAARD.MTH.PDX.EDU 4000
JHM	vesuvius.ccs.neu.edu 1709
Jurassic Weyr	ADAMWEST.INS.CWRU.EDU 6250
KallistiMud	mud.csos.orst.edu 4000
KAOS X	flower.aud.temple.edu 4000
Kender's Kove	harvey.esu.edu 6715
Kingdoms	GWAIHIR.DD.CHALMERS.SE 1812
KoBra	KOBRA.ET.TUDELFT.NL 23
LambdaMOO	LAMBDA.XEROX.COM 8888
Lands of Tabor	snipe.tamucc.edu 9999
Last Outpost	lo.millcomm.com 4000
Legend MUD	sylvester.cc.utexas.edu 9999
Legend of Fire	spider.compart.fi 4066
Legend of the Winds	ccsun44.csie.nctu.edu.tw 4040
Legion MUSH	A.CS.OKSTATE.EDU 2996
Little Italy	ipo.tesi.dsi.unimi.it 4444
Loch Ness	armageddon.imp.ch 2222

continues

MUD	Telnet Address
Looney Mud	looney.cp.tn.tudelft.nl 8888
LopingThrough the Mud	mutt.hamline.edu 9000
Lords of Chaos	rush.cc.edu 1313
LOST Mud	goofy.cc.utexas.edu 6666
Lost Realms	hewey.cs.wmich.edu 6666
LustyMud	LUSTY.TAMU.EDU 2000
MadROM	DOGBERT.UGCS.CALTECH.EDU 1536
Maelstrom 2	144.35.74.240 4000
Marches of Antan	CHECFS2.UCSD.EDU 3000
MarsBase Alpha 4	jumper.mcc.ac.uk 3214
Masquerade	PHOBOS.UNM.EDU 4444
Meat MUD	SNEEZY.CC.UTEXAS.EDU 2800
MediaMOO	purple-crayon.media.mit.edu 8888
Medievia	medievia.netaxs.com 4000
Metaverse	METAVERSE.IO.COM 7777
MiCrOcOsM	fwk098037.res-hall.nwu.edu 6789
MicroMUSE	CHEZMOTO.AI.MIT.EDU 4201
Midnight Sun	HOLLY.LUDD.LUTH.SE 3000
Might, Magic & Mushrooms	prime.mdata.fi 6047
MirrorMOO	everest.ccs.neu.edu 8889
MOOFrancais	logos.daedalus.com 8888
Moonstar	PULSAR.HSC.EDU 4321
MOOsaico	mes03.di.uminho.pt 7777

MUD	Telnet Address
MooseHead Mud	MUD.ESKIMO.COM 4000
Mortal Realms	HYDROGEN.EE.UTULSA.EDU 4321
Mozart	Kitten.mcs.com 4500
Mud with No Name	aviator.cc.iastate.edu 2020
MUD 2 at SONet	193.119.96.1
Muddog	catalyst.math.ufl.edu 2000
Muddy waters	HOT.CALTECH.EDU 3000
MUD II at IPlay	199.182.210.2
Mulberry Mud	lunch.ecst.csuchico.edu 2032
MuMOO	CHESTNUT.ENMU.EDU 7777
Mustang	MUSTANG.US.DELL.COM 9173
MysticAdventure	miniac.etu.gel.ulaval.ca 4000
NAILS	FLOUNDER.RUTGERS.EDU 5150
NamelessMUSH	OCCAMS.DFCI.HARVARD.EDU 6666
NANVAENT3	corrour.cc.strath.ac.uk 3000
NarniaMUSH	DOBEST.LIB.VIRGINIA.EDU 6250
NecroMOO	cyberion.musenet.org 4242
NeverEnding Story	snowhite.ee.pdx.edu 9999
New Hercules MUD	SUNSHINE.EUSHC.ORG 3000
Newmoon	JOVE.CS.PDX.EDU 7680
NightMare	nightmare.imaginary.com 1701
Nirvana 4	ELOF.ACC.IIT.EDU 3500

continues

MUD	Telnet Address
No Known Reality	hopi.dtcc.edu 4000
Northern Crossroads	UGSPARC13.EECG.TORONTO.EDU 9000
Northern Lights	ABER.LUDD.LUTH.SE 6715
Nuclear War	MELBA.ASTRAKAN.HGS.SE 23
OpalMUD	OPAL.CS.VIRGINIA.EDU 4000
Overdrive	CASTOR.ACS.OAKLAND.EDU 5195
PaderMUD	mud.uni-paderborn.de 3000
Paradox	ADL.UNCC.EDU 10478
Patternfall	MISC.ACF.NYU.EDU 4444
Perilous Realms	PR.MESE.COM 23
PernMUSH	astral.magic.ca 4201
Phantazm	FPA.COM 4000
Phidar	phidar.traveller.com 9000
Phoenix	ALBERT.BU.EDU 3500
PMC MOO	HERO.VILLAGE.VIRGINIA.EDU 7777
PowerStruggle	harrier.forsmark.uu.se 3000
PrairieMUSH	FIREFLY.PRAIRIENET.ORG 4201
PrimalMud	JEACK.APANA.ORG.AU 4000
Primenet	boingo.primenet.com 4000
Psycho-thriller	ATLANTIS.EDU 3000
PuRgAtorY	jaxnet.JAXNET.COM 2112
QUOVADIS	mud.imp.ch 2345
Ragnarok	ragnarok.teleport.com 2222

MUD	Telnet Address
Realm of Magic	P107.INFORMATIK.UNI-BREMEN.DE 4000
Realms of the Dragon	cw-u04.umd.umich.edu 3000
RealmsMUCK	TCP.COM 7765
Realmsmud	realms.dorsai.org 1501
Revenge of the End of the Line	AUS.STANFORD.EDU 2010
Rhostshyl	RHOSTSHYL.CIT.CORNELL.EDU 4201
RivaMUSH	ETHERLANDS.YPSI.MI.US 7777
RockyMud	HERMES.DNA.MCI.COM 4000
Rogue	rogue.coe.ohio-state.edu 2222
RoninMUD	Ronin.BCHS.UH.EDU 5000
Sanctuary	pauli.sos.clarkson.edu 9000
Segmentation	concrete.resnet.upenn.edu 4000
Shadowdale	DALE.HSC.UNT.EDU 7777
Shadowrun MUSH	picard.dnaco.net 4201
Shards	VESTA.UNM.EDU 7777
Shattered World	IP1.CS.MONASH.EDU.AU 2666
Shattered Worlds	ip1.cs.monash.edu.au 2666
Silicon Realms	SAMPAN.EE.FIT.EDU 4000
Silver	DANTE.EXIDE.COM 6715
Sleepless Nights	CS3.BROOKES.AC.UK 6789
SlothMUD	AI.CS.UKANS.EDU 6101
SlothMUD II	ai.cs.ukans.edu 6101

continues

MUD	Telnet Address
Sojourn	menzo.sojourn.com 9999
SouCon	BEECHNUT.ENMU.EDU 4201
SpamMUD	ganymede.ics.uci.edu 5000
SplitSecond	lestat.shv.hb.se 3000
SplitSecond	LESTAT.SHV.HB.SE 3000
StackMUD	MARCEL.STACKEN.KTH.SE 8000
StarMOO	asimov.elk-grove.k12.il.us 6879
Starmud	starmud.solace.mh.se 4000
Stick in the MUD	UGSPARC11.EECG.UTORONTO.CA 9000
StickMUD	stickmud.jyu.fi 7680
StrikeNet	mozart.fin.depaul.edu 4000
STYX	DREAMTIME.NMSU.EDU 3000
Surfers	muscle.rai.kcl.ac.uk 3232
SvenskMUD	BODIL.LYSATOR.LIU.SE 2043
SWmud	Kitten.mcs.com 6666
Sword Quest	KENNEDY.ECN.UOKNOR.EDU 5500
SwordsMUSH	WORLD.STD.COM 4201
SyrinxMOO	cimsun.aidt.edu 2112
T'Mud	WAVE.ST.USM.EDU 2222
Tales of Ta'veren	DELPHI.GLENDON.YORKU.CA 4201
TapestriesMUCK	eith.biostr.washington.edu 2069
TAPPMud	SURPRISE.PRO.UFZ.DE 6510
Tazmania	Ukko.Rowan.Edu 5000

MUD	Telnet Address
TerminalGuidance	shire.ncsa.uiuc.edu 6969
Terradome	CMSSRV-GW.BROOKES.AC.UK 8888
Tesseract	mud.ior.com 9000
Texas Twilight MUSH	SEDS.LPL.ARIZONA.EDU 6250
The Castle Greens	prog.mpcs.com 6060
The DAMNED	JANUS.LIBRARY.CMU.EDU 6250
The Edge of Darkness	edge.uccs.edu 2001
The Enchanted Realms	hoplink.com 3000
The Final Challenge	mud.primenet.com 4000
The Glass Dragon	SURF.TSTC.EDU 4000
The Holy Mission	alijku05.edvz.uni-linz.ac.at 2001
The Idea Exchange	imaginary.com 7890
The Land of Drogon	frink.meiko.com 6123
The Mud With No Name	AVIATOR.CC.IASTATE.EDU 2020
The Pattern	epsilon.me.chalmers.se 6047
The Razor's Edge	spodbox.ehche.ac.uk 4000
The Realm of Doth	lunch.ecst.csuchico.edu 2042
The Round Table	DARASIA.CHEM.WFU.EDU 2222
The Storyteller Circle	DRACO.UNM.EDU 6666
The Void	rosebud.umiacs.umd.edu 4000
TheCocteauMUD	xnet.com 8888
ThunderDome	TDOME.MONTANA.COM 5555

continues

MUD	Telnet Address
TimeMuse	MURREN.AI.MIT.EDU 4201
Timewarp	QUARK.GMI.EDU 5150
TinyCWRU	CAISR2.CAISR.CWRU.EDU 4201
TinyTIM	yay.tim.org 5440
TinyTim	MYELIN.UCHC.EDU 5440
TMI-2	KENDALL.CCS.NEU.EDU 5555
TooMUSH 4	occams.dfci.harvard.edu 7777
ToonMUSH III	BRAHE.PHYS.UNM.EDU 9999
TOS TrekMuse	mill2.millcomm.com 1701
Transformers	megavolt.cc.vt.edu 4201
TrekMOO	trekmoo.microserve.com 2499
TrekMUSE	LAUREL.CNIDR.ORG 1701
TrippyMUSH	PEBKAC.SATELNET.ORG 7567
TrollzMUD	ouray.denver.colorado.edu 9000
Tron	polaris.king.ac.uk 3000
TubMUD	MORGEN.CS.TU-BERLIN.DE 768
Two Moons Mush	LUPINE.ORG 4201
Ultima8	RKW-RISC.CS.UP.AC.ZA 1984
Ultimate	rkw-risc.cs.up.ac.za 1984
Unbridled Desires	EPONA.MAGIBOX.NET 8888
UNITOPIA	HELPDESK.RUS.UNI-STUTTGART.DE 3333
University of MOO	moo.cs.uwindsor.ca 7777
Unknown MUD	next5.cas.muohio.edu 5000

MUD	Telnet Address
UNNAMED MUD	screewee.ee.up.ac.za 4000
Utopia	ALPHA.DSU.EDU 6789
V-Muck	MSERV.WIZVAX.COM 520
Valhalla	VALHALLA.COM 2444
Valhalla MUD	marcel.stacken.kth.se 4242
ValhallaMOO	VALHALLA.ACUSD.EDU 4444
VegaMuse II	PLANCK.SOS.CLARKSON.EDU 2095
VertigoMUD	vertigo.apana.org.au 2001
VieMUD	gale.cs.odu.edu 4000
VikingMUD	viking.pvv.unit.no 2001
Virtual World of Magma	magma.leg.ufrj.br 4000
VirtualChicago	chicago.ripco.com 4201
WackoMUSH	RED-BRANCH.MIT.EDU 6003
Wayne's World	DRAKE.EUSHC.ORG 9000
Wildside	LEVANT.CS.OHIOU.EDU 1234
WindsMare	cyberion.bbn.com 7348
Windy Mud	bitsy.apana.org.au 2000
WizMUCK	MSERV.WIZVAX.COM 4201
Wonderland	gorina3.hsr.no 3287
Worlds of Carnage	orcrist.digital.ufl.edu 4000
WriteMUSH	PALMER.SACC.COLOSTATE.EDU 6250
Your MUD Name Here	solo.cc.emory.edu 6666

continues

MUD	Telnet Address
Zebedee	rszircon.swan.ac.uk 7000
ZenMOO	CHESHIRE.OXY.EDU 7777
ZombieMUD	linux1.sjoki.uta.fi 3333

Lagniappe:
A Wedding in Cyberspace

The author, in his Net travels for this book, was lucky enough to happen upon the following blissful, public, event at Northern Lights—a uniting of characters on a MUD. Here's a (heavily abridged) capture file of the happy proceedings. (Whether the commitment made this day extended beyond the bounds of the MUD and the characters involved could not be determined.)

```
The Village Church
    You are in the village's small wooden church. A gentle breeze blows into
the church, disturbing the dust that dances in the sunbeams that shine faintly
through the windows. A doorway leads south.
    At your feet a huge sacrificial pit allows you to give valuables to the gods
in the hope of being rewarded.
```

[The guests arrive.]

```
Boxy has arrived.
Boxy smiles happily.
Henos has arrived.
EV has arrived.
EV places his cloak on the ground, lies down, and begins to sleep.
Kylie has entered the game.
Kylie waves happily.
Tomar has arrived.
```

(The groom, Hawke, arrives.)

```
Icculus rummages through his backpack.
Aleyn sends Hawke a rose.
Wildflower raises an eyebrow.
EV flies around the room.
Rook gasps in astonishment!
```

```
Guin has entered the game.
With a large crash of thunder, Hawke has arrived.
Hawke smiles happily.
MajorTom cheers Hawke on.
Sabkha hugs Hawke.
MajorTom hugs Hawke.
EV cheers Hawke on.
Hawke hugs Sabkha.
Delphina sends Hawke a rose.
Hawke smiles at MajorTom.
Trevie sends Hawke a rose.
Hawke sends Delphina a rose.
Nichole hugs Hawke.
Hawke sends Trevie a rose.
Wildflower has a headache.
Corona comforts Wildflower, and offers her sympathy.
Hawke smiles at Corona.
Wildflower thanks Corona wholeheartedly.
Corona stares dreamily at Hawke.
Trevie cheers Hawke on and congratulates him on his success.
Hawke thanks Nichole wholeheartedly.
Wildflower twiddles her thumbs.
Hawke smiles happily.
Hawke humms and umms in deep thoughts.
Sabkha hands Hawke a hot cup of tea.
Hawke smiles at Sabkha.
*POOF!* Syylk teleports merrily beside you.
A landing party has been beamed down, and Absolon is one of them.
A flash of lightning hits the branch where Hawke was sitting.
```

[Guests are transported to the ceremony.]

```
You are summoned by Hawke.

Sacred Clearing
   You find yourself in a clearing deep in the Misty Mountains. Some mighty
being has carved this niche out of the living rock, making a place suitable for
the gods themselves to wed. A simple podium in the center of this clearing
lends to the overall impression that this is a holy place.
   Stands have been hewn out of the mountain and intricately carved with an
animal motif. Each of the 50 seats depicts a different creature, and all
appear calm and serene.
   A feeling of peace and goodwill washes over you as you gaze in awe at the
majestic peaks that surround this place.
A necklace adorned with a faintly gleaming gem lies here.
A black tuxedo has been carefully hung from a peg here.
A dress with the same blue colour as summer nights, has been left here.
Someone has left a wonderful green dress here.
No Limits...No Boundaries is here.
Absolon has many windows... PLEASE BEEP :) is sitting here.
Concordia Wolvesbane, The Storm Queen is here.
La Dolce Vitastjern is here.
```

EsseX **[the bride]** is here.

A very large Hawke is here.
Iguana appears, looking bewildered.
Vitastjern takes the necklace.

[Vitastjern is the top wizard.]

Hawke takes the tuxedo.
Ramoth shouts 'anyone need a lift to the wedding?'
Hawke wears the tuxedo.
EsseX thanks Vitastjern wholeheartedly.
MajorTom appears with an ear-splitting bang.
Jenn floats down out of the Sky on her magic cloud.
Jules appears, looking bewildered.
Clara appears, looking bewildered.
Bella flies in on her winged horse.
A mighty horn blast echoes around you.
Nichole appears, looking bewildered.
Jenn curtseys gracefully.
Concordia examines the sunglasses closely.
Gusts appears, looking bewildered.
POOF! Syylk teleports merrily besides you.
Vitastjern takes the tuxedo.
The sun hides behind a thickening layer of clouds.
Boxy appears, looking bewildered.
Gusts sits down.
Syylk waves happily.
Sabkha appears, looking bewildered.
GreyJew sighs loudly.
GreyJew sits down.
A green shimmer fills the place, and ErIC appears!
Rook appears, looking bewildered.
Corona appears, looking bewildered.
Aleyn appears, looking bewildered.
Jenn smiles happily.
A HUGE MUSHROOM CLOUD ERUPTS BEFORE YOU...Jerry walks out smiling
Corona sits down.
Guzman gives Jules the dress.
Rook sits down.
Corona raises her hand in greeting and says 'Hello!'
Hawke smiles at Jerry.
Aleyn sits down.
Hawke smiles at Corona.
Concordia wears the sunglasses.
Hawke is beaming so brightly. What could be the source?
Corona raises her hand in greeting and says 'Hello!'
Doc has transported himself here. He was aiming for the men's room.
Tears of joy have formed in Corona's eyes as she smiles happily round the room.
CALL FOR ARRIVAL BY Morpheus: I have arrived.
Syylk bows to Hawke.
Rook lets loose a bloodcurdling howl at the moon.
Aleyn hiccups drunkedly.
ErIC says 'We have a slight problem here...'

Corona hugs everyone!!
MajorTom raises an eyebrow.
Vitastjern nods to ErIC in agreement.
ErIC says 'We lost the officiator somewhere in the voids...'
GreyJew nods to ErIC in agreement.
Corona listens carefully as ErIC talks.
ErIC smirks.
GreyJew says 'No Ozy?'
Jerry greedily devours the beer.
Fisherman arrives.
Corona sighs loudly.
Bella says 'nope..Ozy's gone, missing'
Aleyn burps loudly.
Biff arrives.
Jenn stares into space.
ErIC smiles happily.
MajorTom sends Bonkers a rose.
Rook whimpers quietly in the corner.
Hawke smiles at Rook.
Vitastjern says 'Listen up now, please be quiet so we can get the ceremony started, ok?'
Biff nips at your heels.
Jerry burps loudly.
Ramoth nods solemnly.
Rook growls at Biff.
Iguana sits down.
Biff wags his tail.
Ramoth sits down.
Hawke sends Boone a rose.
Ramoth giggles in a fit of uncontrollable mirth.
ErIC sets the NoRose flag on the room.
The dress vanishes, summoned by EsseX!
Concordia lifts an eyebrow behind her dark shades and says 'COOL!'
Magically, a hole opens in the ground and Robi jumps up!
A voice shouts 'BRYN MAWR ROCKS!'
A voice shouts 'bryn mawr rocks rock!'
GreyJew sighs loudly.
Rook shakes his head.
A voice shouts 'and we do rock men's cages!'
Vitastjern says 'I am going to do the ceremony, but since'
GreyJew thanks Vitastjern wholeheartedly.
Vitastjern says 'I am in a hurry, please keep quiet.'
A voice shouts 'YES WE DO!!!!....watch out!'
Ramoth nods to Vitastjern in agreement.
Vitastjern says 'No emotes, no actions until the ceremony is over, ok?'
Bella nods solemnly.
Hendricks shouts 'cages?'
Nichole nods solemnly.
Vitastjern says 'And no shouts, Hendricks.'
A voice shouts 'ok...rock their socks then.'
Bonkers appears, looking bewildered.
Aleyn hiccups drunkenly.
Syylk nods solemnly.
Concordia takes her place and waits.
Vitastjern fetches something from another dimension.

Vitastjern wears the robe.
Vitastjern fetches something from another dimension.
Hawke shouts 'do any mortals who are not already here want to come to the wedding?'
The bright light of day is replaced by the gentle twilight of evening.
Sabkha cheers Hawke on.
With an eruption of gasoline and guitar, Hendricks has arrived!
Anne appears, looking bewildered.
Vitastjern says 'Please be as quiet as you can during the ceremony.'
Anita appears, looking bewildered.
Vitastjern steps up to the altar.
Vitastjern smiles warmly and says 'I'm happy to greet you all. Welcome to
Celine appears, looking bewildered.
The gibbous moon comes out of the clouds.
Anne places her arm around Hendricks.
Vitastjern says 'this joyful event where Hawke and EsseX will be joined in a'
Someone hugs Celine.
Vitastjern says 'MUDmarriage.'
Jerry hiccups drunkenly.
Jerry cringes in terror!
Vitastjern turns to the bride and the groom and smiles warmly.
Hendricks places his guitar at the door.
EsseX haS aRriVeD aNd iS reAdY tO cAuSe miSchieF.
Reeda appears, looking bewildered.
Vitastjern says 'Hawke and EsseX, if you please step forward.'
Hendricks drops the burntguitar.
Hawke smiles happily.
EsseX falls down laughing.
EsseX says 'Suppose I should be here :)'
Anne winks at Hendricks.
Vitastjern giggles in a fit of uncontrollable mirth.
Hawke steps forward.
Jerry stumbles drunkenly around.
Jerry looks more sober now.
Concordia nods solemnly.
Vitastjern says 'EsseX? Step forward please.'
EsseX steps forward With hawKE.
Vitastjern says 'Who will act as best man for the groom?'
Morpheus waves happily.
Morpheus says 'erm, that would be me!'
Hawke looks at Morpheus.
Hawke smiles at Morpheus.
Morpheus searches for the ring... "No, not in this pocket...", "Not in this one
either *panic*", 'Aaah! In my left shoe!'
Anne rummages through her backpack.
Hendricks says 'eww'
Vitastjern says 'And who will be the maid for the bride?'
Anne says 'I will'
EsseX cheers Anne on.
ErIC smiles happily.
Anne steps forward.
Hendricks gooses Anne.
Celine smiles at Anne.
Hendricks says 'get up there woman'
Anne says 'I have darling'

Anne curtseys gracefully.
Vitastjern clears her throat.
Peloquin sits down.
Morpheus stares dreamily at EsseX.
Vitastjern says 'If there is anyone among you who see any reason why Hawke and'
Boone sits down.
Vitastjern says 'EsseX should not be joined in MUD marriage, speak up now, or for
Vitastjern says 'ever hold your peace.'
Morpheus humms and umms in deep thoughts.
Absolon humms and umms in deep thoughts.
MajorTom humms and umms in deep thoughts.
Hendricks ponders the question of life, universe and everything.
Anne thinks everyone better SHUT THEIR MOUTHS.
Morpheus grins at EsseX!
Vitastjern says 'Stop the scrolling please.'
Hendricks is thinking about wildflowers.
Concordia agrees with anne...
Wildflower appears, looking bewildered.
Vitastjern turns to Hawke and smiles.
Hawke smiles at Vitastjern.
Vitastjern says 'Do you, Hawke, take EsseX as your beloved MUDwife,'
Vitastjern says 'from now to ever after?'
Anne bursts into tears.
Sabkha bursts into tears.
Hawke says 'i do. :)'
The glorious sunset is over. Night settles on the sleepy land.
Celine bursts into tears.
Absolon bursts into tears.
Morpheus stares into space.
Anne sobs.
EsseX wonders why everyone is crazy.
Celine sniffs.
EsseX shakes her hand.
Vitastjern turns to EsseX and smiles to her.
Concordia sighs happily.
EsseX says 'Just cause i'm a legend :P'
Peloquin puts on his wellingtons.
Boone sobs.
Anne throws back her head and cackles with glee!
EsseX smiles happily.
Nichole bursts into tears.
EsseX smiles at Vitastjern.
Hendricks says 'shh, Anne.'
Vitastjern says 'And do you, EsseX, take Hawke as your beloved MUDhusband,'
Nichole sniffs.
Vitastjern says 'from now to ever after?'
EsseX says 'i do, indeedy'
Vitastjern turns to the best man and motions him to give the ring to the groom.
Anne giggles in a fit of uncontrollable mirth.
Corona sobs.
Morpheus scratches his head.
Morpheus gives Hawke the ring.
Nichole sniffs.
Hawke smiles at Morpheus.

Morpheus smiles happily.
Boone comforts Corona, and offers her sympathy.
Celine sobs.
Kalzar is suddenly standing in front of you.
Vitastjern says 'Place the ring on EsseX's finger, Hawke, and say after me'
Anne cries on Hendricks' shoulder
Rook sniffs.
Hawke smiles happily.
EsseX holds out her finger
Hawke gives EsseX the ring.
Concordia smiles broadly
EsseX wears the ring.
Vitastjern says 'I, Hawke,'
Hawke says 'i, hawke'
You hear the cheering of the crowd as someone expertly plays the Jailhouse Rock.
Vitastjern says 'take you, EsseX,'
Hawke says 'take you, EsseX'
Vitastjern says 'as my lawful MUDwife,'
Hawke says 'as my lawful MUDwife'
Vitastjern says 'to have and to hold'
Hawke says 'to have and to hold'
Vitastjern says 'in good adventures and bad'
Hawke says 'in good adventures and bad'
Vitastjern says 'from now until eternal time.'
Hawke says 'from now until eternal time.'
Vitastjern turns to the maid and motions her to give the ring to the bride.
Anne gives EsseX the ring.
Anne grins broadly.
Vitastjern says 'Put the ring on Hawke's finger, EsseX'
Hawke holds out his finger.
GreyJew cries 'Ack! Modem!' and disappears into nothingness.
EsseX gives Hawke the ring.
Hawke wears the ring.
Vitastjern says 'Please repeat after me, EsseX'
Hawke is beaming so brightly. What could be the source?
Vitastjern says 'I, EsseX'
EsseX says 'I, EsseX'
Vitastjern says 'take you, Hawke,'
EsseX says 'Take you, hawke'
Vitastjern says 'as my lawful MUDhusband,'
EsseX says 'as my lawful MUDhusband'
Vitastjern says 'to have and to hold'
Morpheus sniffs.
EsseX says 'to have and to hold'
Vitastjern says 'in good adventures and in bad'
The gibbous moon hides behind a thickening layer of clouds.
EsseX says 'in good adventures and bad.'
Vitastjern says 'from now until eternal time.'
EsseX says 'from now until eternal time.'
Morpheus bursts into tears.
Vitastjern lowers her staff of office to touch the two rings.
Anne sobs.
Vitastjern says 'With the power my office as Goddess at Northern Lights grants me,'
Wildflower dabs at her eyes

Vitastjern says 'I hereby pronounce you MUDhusband and MUD wife.'
Concordia sniffs
Vitastjern says 'You may kiss the bride.'
Morpheus wipes his nose with his Kleenex..
Syylk bursts into tears.
Bella cheers with great gusto!
Nichole sniffs.
Anne cheers with great gusto!
Hawke is beaming so brightly. What could be the source?
Hendricks claps wildly!
Jenn sniffs.
Morpheus sniffs.
Wildflower cheers with great gusto!
Boone has left the game.
A shower of rose petals falls softly down over the happy couple.
Ramoth cheers with great gusto!
Rook bursts into tears.
Celine claps wildly!
Anne cheers with great gusto!
Concordia claps wildly!
Ramoth cheers with great gusto!
Rook lets loose a bloodcurdling howl at the moon.
Hawke gives EsseX a deep and passionate kiss.
Nichole cheers with great gusto!
Hendricks whistles appreciatively.
Anne cheers with great gusto!
MajorTom claps wildly!
A shower of rose petals falls softly down over the happy couple.
Clara makes a silly face and goes 'Awwww...'
Ramoth cheers with great gusto!
Aleyn cheers with great gusto!
Morpheus bursts into tears.
Nichole claps wildly!
Bella claps wildly!
Jenn claps wildly!
Rook lets loose a blood curdling howl at the moon.
>You clap wildly!
Hendricks faints dead away.
Anne shouts 'WOO HOO!'
MajorTom cheers with great gusto!
Jenn cheers with great gusto!
Vitastjern cheers with great gusto!
Tomar claps wildly!
Kalzar cheers Hawke on.
Concordia hugs everyone
Corona takes pictures for the scrapbook!
Hendricks plays a rip on his guitar.
Boxy cheers with great gusto!
Anne throws rice
Guzman cheers with great gusto!
You see the first beams of morning sun break across the eastern horizon.
Hawke gives EsseX a deep and passionate kiss.
Corona shakes hands with Hawke.
Anne kisses EsseX lightly on the cheek!

```
Anne hugs EsseX.
Hawke smiles at Vitastjern.
Hawke waves happily.
EsseX waves happily.
Vitastjern hugs EsseX.
Anne says 'time for the HONEYMOON'
Tears of joy have formed in Corona's eyes as she smiles happily around the room.
Anne cheers with great gusto!
Morpheus grabs his sides and tumbles to the floor in hysterics!
Hendricks says 'cripes...now let those two alone to do what they need to do ;)'
Bella hugs Vitastjern.
Vitastjern says 'Bye everyone!'
Corona hugs Vitastjern.
Vitastjern waves happily.
Vitastjern fades out of existence; not even her footprints can be seen.
>quit
Saving Clortho.


-=-=-=-=-=-=-=-=-=-=-=-=-=-=-=-=-=-=-=-=-=-=-=-=-=-=-=-=-=-=-=-=-=-=-=-=-=-=-=-

                     Leaving the realm of the Northern Lights

-=-=-=-=-=-=-=-=-=-=-=-=-=-=-=-=-=-=-=-=-=-=-=-=-=-=-=-=-=-=-=-=-=-=-=-=-=-=-=-
```

Index

C

Callas, Jon, 36, 147

Camden-Burlington Packet Radio Association, 18–19

cd (change directory) command, 56

CERT (Computer Emergency Response Team), 148

Channels
directory of, with IRC **/list command**, 110–111
operator powers, 104

character case, FTP, 59

Chat channels, on MUD system, 96

Classes, defined, 99

Client/server
functions of, 61–62
IRC and, 107
LPmud for DOS, 132–134

Commands
on IRC systems, 110–117
/away, 116
/dcc, 117
/help, 110
/ignore, 116, 125
/invite, 115, 125
/join, 113, 125
/kick, 117, 125
/list, 110–111, 125
minimizing/list, 111–113
/mode, 114–115, 125
/msg, 114, 126
/names, 116, 126

/part, 117, 126
/query, 116, 125
/quit, 117, 126
/reply, 114, 126
"talk," 113
/topic, 114, 126
/whois, 116, 126
/whowas, 116, 126
on MUD systems
communication commands, 94–99
help command, 88–89
interactive help, 89–90
navigation commands, 90–94

Commercial concerns about the Internet, 145–147

Communication commands
on MUD system, 94–99
page, 95
say, 94–95
shout, 96
tell or whisper, 95

Communications software, MUD access and, 5–6

CompuServe, history of Internet and, 29

Computer-Mediated Communication Magazine, 36–37

Computer resources, for MUD systems, 4

Computer Shopper, 5

Confidentiality
on IRC, 105–106
MUD registration and, 87

crackers, MUD attacks by, 79–80

FTP (File Transfer Protocol)
    characteristics of, 53–55
    clientserver and, 62–63
    command summary, 61
    compression and archiving, 59–61
    long file names, 59
    MUC client access, 131–132
    MUD client program, 62
    PICS Online!, 19–20
    sample facility, 55–59
FurryMUCK, 45
Fur systems, 45

G

Games, Steve Jackson, 37
Gender identity, harassment on MUD and, 71–73
Gibson, William, 45
gifs (graphics files), 58
Goals on MUD systems, 99–100
@go command, MOO systems, 137
Gods and wizards on a MUD, 71–74
GohsMUSH environment, 75–78
Gopher, MUD access with, 81–84
GOTHAMMUD, 46
Graffiti, on Internet Relay Chat (IRC), 104
graphics-based MUDs, 49–50
GUI (graphical user interface)
    Pipeline Access and, 20–21
Guest logons, 51

H

Hacker Crackdown, The, 35–36, 103
Hamilton, Jacqueline, 42–44
Hand, Chris, 36–37, 146
Harassment on MUDs, 71–73
Hard tail harassment on MUD, 71
Hardware requirements, MUD systems, 8
Harper's Tale MOO, 42, 45
Help command
    commands listed under, 88–89
    MUD registration, 87
/help command, on IRC systems, 110
HoloMUCK, 44
HyperText Markup Language (HTML) format
    Pipeline Access and, 21–22
    World Wide Web and, 65

I

/ignore command, on IRC systems, 116, 125
IIMO (Internet is My Oyster), 21–22
Illuminati Online, 37
In character (IC) behavior, 69, 74
Incompatible Timesharing System (ITS), 27
Infocom, ZORK game series, 30
Interactive fiction, 30
Interactive help command, 89–90
Internav, on Delphi, 22–23
Internet, increased consciousness of, 35–36

M

Magic user class, 99

Mail command, on MUD system.
    See MUDmail

mail doors, in Usenets, 64

McCaffrey, Ann, 45

MediaMOO system, 134–135

Meeting Space (business MUD), 37–38, 147

Metaverse system, 37

MilMUDs, 41

minimizing/list command, on IRC systems,
    111–113

Mize, William, 45–47

Moberg, Vic, 41

Mobiles (class/race), 99

mode command, on IRC systems,
    114–115, 125

Modems (MODulator/DEModulator)
    defined, 4–5
    history of, 27

MOOgramming, 134

MOO (MUD Object-oriented) systems
    characteristics of, 2, 34, 132–134
    commands for, 137–140
    @create command, 139–140
    @describe command, 136
    editing verbs for, 141–144
    educational applications, 39–40
    @examine command, 138
    @go command, 136–137
    living space, 135
    LPmud for DOS, 133–134
    Metaverse as example of, 37

@parent command, 139

@recycle command, 136–137

@sethome command, 135

verbs for, 140–144

Morse, Samuel F. P., 25

MS-DOS systems, MUD access with, 8

/msg command, on IRC systems, 114, 126

MUD attack, 69

MUD clients, defined, 50, 61–62

"Mudding: Social Phenomena in Text-Based
    Virtual Realities," 71–72

MUD FAQ, 127

MUD II, exit commands, 91–94

MUD/IRC newsgroups, 64

Mudlib, 128–129

MUDlist, 168–184

MUDmail command, 96

MUDman, LP mud for DOS, 131–132

MUD parser, LPmud for DOS, 130

MUDserver, access to MUD addresses, 84–86

MUD systems
    access to, 3–4, 81
    BBS as route to, 5
    behavioral standards, 69
    commands on, 88–99. *See also* entries
      under specific commands
    communications/terminal software, 5–6
    computer resources for, 4
    data compression, 6
    defined, 1
    Delphi access, 22–23, 81–84
    diversification of MUD programs, 35

N

O

S

SAGE air warning radar system, 25–27

Say command, on MUD system, 94–95

Scanner/cleaner software, 7

Scoping telephone services, directory of, 12–17

Scripts, on IRC systems, 117–118

secret mode (+/-s), on IRC systems, 115, 125

Security measures
    on Internet, 147–148
    on IRC, 104–105
    on MUDs registration and, 86–87

serious MUDs, 1

@sethome command, MOO system, 135

Shareware, for MUD systems, 6

Shout command, on MUD system, 96

Site addresses
    FTPs, 55
    Telnet, 51

Site instability, in MUD systems, 42–43

Smith, Jennifer, 62, 127, 153

Social MUDs
    commands on, 100
    defined, 1
    history of, 32–33

Sonet, 33

SouCon MUSH, attack on, 79–80

Spacewar (MIT), 30

Spatial metaphor, MUD communication commands, 94

Spells commands, 99

SPRINGFIELD MUD, 46

SprintNet PDN, 8, 24
    Pipeline Access and, 20–21

#starfleet channel, 118

Sterling, Bruce, 35, 103

Steve Jackson Games, 37

Stibitz, George R., 25

System operators (sysops), 7

T

"talk" command, on IRC systems, 113

tar UNIX program, file compression and archiving, 60

TCP/IP (Transmission Control Protocol/ Internet Protocol) agreements
    defined, 2, 50
    security concerns, 148
    UNIX development and, 29

Technology requirements, MUD access and, 8

Telephone service, MUD access and, 7–8

Tell command, on MUD system, 94–95

Tell or whisper command, 95

Telnet
    defined, 2, 17, 50–51
    sample sites, 51–53

Terminal software, MUD access and, 5–6

TextSpace, 37–38

Textual environments, 1

threads, on Usenets, 63–64

Time sharing, history of the Internet and, 27

TinyMUD, history of, 34

TIW (Toe in the Water) plan, 21–22

NOTES

NOTES

NOTES

Available Now!

1-2-3 for Windows: The Visual Learning Guide	$19.95
ACT! 2.0: The Visual Learning Guide	$19.95
Windows Magazine Presents: Access from the Ground Up	$19.95
The CD-ROM Revolution	$24.95
CompuServe Information Manager for Windows: The Complete Membership Kit & Handbook (with two 3 ½" disks)	$29.95
Computers Don't Byte	$7.95
Computer Gamer's Survival Guide	$19.95
CorelDRAW! 4 Revealed!	$24.95
CorelDRAW! 4 for Windows By Example (with 3 ½" disk)	$34.95
CorelDRAW! 5 Revealed!	$24.95
Create Wealth with Quicken	$19.95
Cruising America Online: The Visual Learning Guide	$19.95
Excel 5 for Windows By Example (with 3 ½" disk)	$29.95
Excel 5 for Windows: The Visual Learning Guide	$19.95
Excel for the Mac: The Visual Learning Guide	$19.95
Free Electronic Networks	$24.95
WINDOWS Magazine Presents: Freelance Graphics for Windows: The Art of Presentation	$27.95
Harvard Graphics for Windows: The Art of Presentation	$27.95
Internet After Hours	$19.95
Internet for Windows—America Online Edition: The Visual Learning Guide	$19.95
KidWare: The Parent's Guide to Software for Children	$14.95
Lotus Notes 3 Revealed!	$24.95
LotusWorks 3: Everything You Need to Know	$24.95
Mac Tips and Tricks	$14.95
Making Movies with Your PC	$24.95
Microsoft Office in Concert	$24.95
Microsoft Office in Concert, Professional Edition	$27.95
Microsoft Works for Windows By Example	$24.95

OS/2 WARP: Easy Installation Guide	$12.95
PageMaker 4.2 for the Mac: Everything You Need to Know	$19.95
PageMaker 5 for the Mac: Everything You Need to Know	$24.95
PageMaker 4.0 for Windows: Everything You Need to Know	$19.95
PageMaker 5 for Windows: Everything You Need to Know	$19.95
Paradox for DOS Revealed! (with 3 ½" disk)	$29.95
Paradox for Windows Essential Power Programming (with 3 ½" disk)	$39.95
A Parent's Guide to Video Games	$12.95
PC DOS 6.2: Everything You Need to Know	$24.95
PowerPoint: The Visual Learning Guide	$19.95
WINDOWS Magazine Presents: The Power of Windows and DOS Together, Second Edition	$24.95
Quicken for Windows: The Visual Learning Guide	$19.95
Quicken 3 for Windows: The Visual Learning Guide	$19.95
QuickTime: Making Movies with Your Macintosh, Second Edition	$27.95
The Slightly Skewed Computer Dictionary	$8.95
Smalltalk Programming for Windows (with 3 ½" disk)	$39.95
The Software Developers Complete Legal Companion (with 3 ½" disk)	$32.95
Software: What's Hot! What's Not!	$16.95
Superbase Revealed!	$29.95
SuperPaint 3: Everything You Need to Know	$24.95
Think THINK C! (with two 3 ½" disks)	$39.95
Thom Duncan's Guide to NetWare Shareware (with 3 ½" disk)	$29.95
Visual Basic for Applications Revealed!	$27.95
The Warp Book: Your Definitive Guide to Installing and Using OS/2 v3	$24.95
Windows 3.1: The Visual Learning Guide	$19.95
WinFax PRO 4: The Visual Learning Guide	$19.95
Word for Windows 2: The Visual Learning Guide	$19.95
Word for Windows 6: The Visual Learning Guide	$19.95
WordPerfect 6 for DOS By Example	$24.95
WordPerfect 6 for DOS: How Do I . . .?	$24.95
WordPerfect 6 for DOS: The Visual Learning Guide	$19.95
WordPerfect 6 for Windows By Example	$29.95
WordPerfect 6 for Windows: How Do I...?	$24.95
WordPerfect 6 for Windows: The Visual Learning Guide	$19.95

8/95 1

To Order Books

Please send me the following items:

Quantity	Title	Unit Price	Total
_____	_____	$ _____	$ _____
_____	_____	$ _____	$ _____
_____	_____	$ _____	$ _____
_____	_____	$ _____	$ _____
_____	_____	$ _____	$ _____
_____	_____	$ _____	$ _____

Subtotal	$ _____
7.25% Sales Tax (CA only)	$ _____
8.25% Sales Tax (TN only)	$ _____
5.0% Sales Tax (MD only)	$ _____
7.0% G.S.T. Canadian Orders	$ _____
Shipping and Handling*	$ _____
Total Order	$ _____

* $4.00 shipping and hand-ling charge for the first book and $1.00 for each additional book.

By Telephone: With MC or Visa, call (916) 632-4400. Mon-Fri, 9-4 PST.

By Mail: Just fill out the information below and send with your remittance to:

Prima Publishing
P.O. Box 1260BK
Rocklin, CA 95677

Satisfaction unconditionally guaranteed.

My name is _____

I live at _____

City _____ State _____ Zip _____

MC/Visa# _____ Exp. _____

Signature _____